ST JOHN'S GOSPEL

Brian Grenier CFC

ST JOHN'S GOSPEL
A self-directed retreat

St Paul Publications

ACKNOWLEDGEMENTS

Scripture texts used in this work are taken from *The New American Bible with Revised New Testament*. Copyright © 1986 by the Confraternity of Christian Doctrine, Washington, DC, and are used by permission of copyright owner. All rights reserved.

Translation of the Magnificat reprinted from *Psalms Anew: In Inclusive Language*, compiled by Nancy Schreck and Maureen Leach. (Winona, MN: Saint Mary's Press, 1986.) Used by permission of the publisher. All rights reserved.

'Imagination and Praying the Gospels' appeared first in *Catholic Schools Studies* (Vol 63, No 2, October 1990) and 'Faith in the Fourth Gospel' appeared first in *Word and Life* (Vol 39, No 1, February 1991).

ST JOHN'S GOSPEL: A self-directed retreat
©Brian Grenier CFC, 1991

First published, October 1991

Cover: Cimabue's painting of St John Evangelist
Cover design: Bruno Colombari SSP

National Library of Australia
Card Number and ISBN 0 949080 46 2

Published by
ST PAUL PUBLICATIONS — Society of St Paul,
60-70 Broughton Road — PO Box 230 — Homebush, NSW 2140

Typeset and printed by Society of St Paul, Wantirna South, Victoria

---

St Paul Publications is an activity of the Priests and Brothers of the Society of St Paul who proclaim the Gospel through the media of social communication

To Charles and Evelyn Grinyer

CONTENTS

Introduction	9
First preparatory reading *John: A different Gospel*	31
Second preparatory reading *Faith in the Fourth Gospel*	49
Third preparatory reading *Imagination and praying the Gospels*	65
Day One *Jesus and Nicodemus*	77
Day Two *Jesus and the Samaritan woman*	103
Day Three *Jesus and the man born blind*	129
Day Four *Jesus and the family at Bethany*	157
Day Five *Jesus and a trio of disciples: Judas, Peter, Thomas*	183
Day Six *Jesus, the mother of Jesus and the beloved disciple*	213
Glossary	239
Bibliography	245

INTRODUCTION

THE PROJECT

My purpose in writing this book is to provide prospective retreatants with suitable reading material for use during the course of a six-days 'do-it-yourself' spiritual renewal experience based on St John's Gospel.

This material focuses each day, in a definite sequence, on one or more of the representative figures of the Gospel. It includes both detailed commentaries on relevant sections of the biblical text and complementary guidelines for contemplative prayer.

Though it is designed primarily for personal use in solitude by men and women who, through necessity or personal preference, plan to enter into a time of retreat without the assistance of a preacher or director, it could easily be adapted to other purposes and could even be used for study and/or reflective reading as the Spirit moves. Moreover, it is sufficiently flexible to admit of effective use in a group situation or, over a period of time, as a series of six single days of recollection.

It presupposes at least some familiarity with modern biblical scholarship; but it is by no means aimed at the specialist reader. My hope is that it will benefit many people who wish to increase their acquaintance with the words of John with a view to knowing more intimately that Word who is his subject.

In an attempt to establish the rationale and the experiential background of my project, there are a number of questions which must now be raised. Why a retreat; why St John's Gospel; why link study and prayer; and why a 'do-it-yourself' approach?

BACKGROUND/RATIONALE

Why a retreat?

For more than two decades, respected sociologists of religion and sundry prophets of doom alike (often lusty of lung but innocent of scholarship) have been pointing to the increasing secularism of society in many parts of the Western World, including my own country, Australia. They adduce as evidence the erosion of moral sensibilities, the falling away of religious practice (usually measured in terms of regular church attendance), and widespread uncertainty or even disillusionment about such basic issues as the meaning, purpose and direction of human existence.

At the same time, however, we are witnessing a very significant resurgence of interest in spirituality which is not confined to any one age group. This resurgence finds expression in the charismatic and other renewal movements, in the formation of new and vibrant faith-sharing communities, in greatly increased enrolments in introductory and advanced courses of scripture and theology, in biblically-based commitment to such causes as peace and justice and responsible stewardship of the environment, and in the making of retreats or similar renewal activities with or without the assistance of a director.

In connection with this last-mentioned item, I can only express, from increasing personal experience in retreat ministry, my complete agreement with the assessment of

Introduction

George (1989:10). 'In all my years in the retreat movement and in working in the spiritual arena of life,' he writes, 'I have never seen a time when the spiritual hunger was as deeply felt as by many people today.'

It may be well at this point to clarify the sense in which the term 'retreat' is used throughout this book. For me it denotes a more or less prolonged and rather structured period of time, deliberately set apart from the affairs of everyday life, in which one's quest for God is intensified and illuminated by means of prayer, personal reflection on one's life-journey, and other appropriate exercises.

The expression, 'deliberately set apart from the affairs of everyday life', is not intended to imply that such affairs are irrelevant to the making of a retreat. Indeed, our own individual concerns and those of our fellow human beings always deserve serious attention both in our reading of the Bible and in our prayer based upon it.

Our model in retreat activity is Jesus himself who, prior to beginning his public ministry, retired into the desert for forty days (Mt 4:1-11 // Mk 1:12-13 // Lk 4:1-13) and who, as St Luke tells us, was accustomed to 'withdraw to deserted places and pray' (Lk 5:16; cf. Mk 1:35). Alone on the Mount of Olives, he would often spend the whole night in prayer to God (cf. Lk 6:12; 21:37-38).

Moreover, Jesus sometimes encouraged his disciples to withdraw with him from the crowds that constantly sought their ministry to a place where they might repose themselves in solitude. 'Come away by yourselves to a deserted place and rest awhile' (Mk 6:3).

With these texts in mind, Townroe (1986:579) quite rightly observes:

> Behind the practice of retreat, and influencing its development in the past and in the present, lies the idea of the desert. The desert in Christian tradition has symbolised the setting in which the traveller, stripped of non-essentials comes face to face with God.

No one appreciated this truth more fully than St Antony (d. 356) and the tens of thousands of men and women who flocked to the deserts of Egypt and Syria in the fourth and fifth centuries to attend to the one thing ultimately necessary (cf. Lk 10:42) and to live the Gospel in a most radical way.

Among Roman Catholics (I write from within that tradition),[1] retreats were generally considered to be for those 'taking the honours course'. They were the preserve of priests and religious (myself among them) who were, and are, required by Canon Law to devote time to them at regular intervals. Unfortunately, there was a strong and enduring tendency for clerical and/or monastic approaches to spirituality, which were presupposed in these exercises, to be imposed on Catholics generally without due regard to their state of life.

The scene has changed remarkably in the decades following the Second Vatican Council. Retreat centres have proliferated, many of them in places highly conducive to reflection on the mystery of human becoming; and the 'clientele' now reflects the quite diverse membership of the faith community as a whole.

The old-style retreat, emphasising personal conversion and preached in an atmosphere of reflective quiet by an ordained minister, is still available to interested Christians of a more traditional bent; but today it is only one offering among many. Increasingly there are retreats, conducted

---

[1] Implicit in the acknowledgement that I speak from a Roman Catholic perspective is the admission that, as is the case with writers (and readers) of all Christian denominations/traditions, I bring to my work certain personal and denominational assumptions. I believe that I have done this in a way which is ecumenically sensitive and which is neither intrusively subjective nor academically untenable. Frequent references to the writings of others across a reasonably broad spectrum of traditions reflects, in part, my consciousness of the limitations of my own preferred perspective.

Introduction

by women and men with suitable expertise, which cater for the spiritual needs of specific groups such as young adults, widows, senior citizens, homosexuals, single parents, university students, the physically disabled, alcoholics and others who suffer from destructively addictive behaviour.

In these retreats there is, not surprisingly, more interaction among the participants and a holistic approach to healing and to personal growth in Christ which seeks to integrate the insights of spirituality and psychology. Recourse may be had not only to scripture and the spiritual classics but also to dream analysis, psychosynthesis, journal writing, the Enneagram and the Myers-Briggs Type Indicator, to name just a few of the currently used techniques.

According to personal preference, many people avail of opportunities to make a rather more private kind of retreat on a one-to-one basis with the help of an experienced director. Others again opt for a style of retreat which reflects a particular spiritual tradition in the life of the Church (for example: Ignatian, Franciscan, Carmelite, charismatic, creation-centred).

The kind of spiritual renewal experience which is offered here is to be seen against this background. It will add to the existing possibilities not a new and highly original paradigm but simply another way of making a retreat — one which I have reason to believe will help to meet the needs expressed by some people whom I have encountered in my ministry.

However, as will be shown in greater detail later, it derives its more immediate inspiration and impetus from my assignment in recent years as a staff member of the international renewal program (tertianship) of the Congregation of Christian Brothers in Rome and from similar involvements with groups of religious sisters. In this context I have been able to trial and to refine, in the light of constructive criticism, most of the material developed in these pages.

Why John's Gospel?

Prior to working in Rome, I was a lecturer for a number of years in the religion department of the Signadou College of Education (Canberra) and the Catholic College of Education (Sydney).[2] During this time my duties included the presentation of courses on St John's Gospel both to undergraduates, most of whom were preparing for teaching careers in Catholic schools, and to graduate students pursuing higher qualifications with a view to specialisation in religious education. As a result of this experience, I developed a deep and special love for the Fourth Gospel.

More to the point, I concluded that 'the spiritual Gospel', as John was referred to quite early in the history of the Christian Church, is particularly well suited for use in a retreat situation because of the sublimity of its teaching and because of the number of one-to-one encounters it contains between Jesus and men and women with whom we can identify in our quest for saving truth.

What is said of Sacred Scripture in general in the Second Vatican Council's Constitution on Divine Revelation (*Dei Verbum* 21) is especially true of St John's Gospel: '[It is] a pure and lasting fount of spiritual life' (Flannery 1975:762).

Why link study and prayer?

It would be easy to respond to this question by observing that, for the Jewish people, the study of the Word of God

---

[2] Both of these institutions, from the beginning of 1991, have been incorporated in the new Australian Catholic University.

Introduction

is itself an act of worship. However, I must draw on my teaching experience once again to justify the inclusion of a strong study component in a spiritual retreat.

Initially, I found that the college students were happy to accept a fairly academic approach to the Gospel; but, as time went by, they increasingly asked for guidance on how one might pray the biblical text — a request consistent with the recommendation of the above mentioned constitution (*Dei Verbum* 25) that 'prayer should accompany the reading of Sacred Scripture' (Flannery 1975:764).

For their part, the tertians in Rome have frequently expressed a wish that their rather more contemplative reading of the same Gospel, under my direction, should be supported by a reasonable amount of scholarly input.

Given the exigencies of time in both of these situations, it was not always easy to strike the right balance. I determined nonetheless that, for the future, I would endeavour to combine prayer and study when dealing with the Gospel, in the belief that one can neither truly comprehend the text without praying it nor pray it as effectively as one might wish without devoting some time to studying it.

Both groups, I might add, emphasised the further need to relate the study of the text and prayer based on it to the everyday concerns of the individual believer and of the wider human community.

Why a 'do-it-yourself' approach?

My work as a college lecturer involved me, from time to time, in what are called, in Australian terminology, 'distance education programs'. These cater for students who live in places remote from the major cities and whose studies are supervised by regular correspondence and supported, where possible, by occasional visits from members of the academic staff.

I have had these people particularly (but not exclusively) in mind in my efforts to design a six-days 'do-it-yourself' Johannine retreat. It became abundantly clear to me that the opportunities for religious study and for the making of retreats, which city-dwellers can so easily take for granted, are simply not available to large numbers of people in such a vast but sparsely populated country as Australia.

It should be noted that, whenever necessity or personal preference dictate that we pray or study the Gospel alone, we should not do so in an individualistic manner; for the Bible is the Church's book. In reading it, we should always be conscious of the gift of faith that we share with other believers. The Church's preferred way of experiencing the Word of God will continue to be the community context provided by liturgical celebrations.

WAYS OF READING THE BIBLE

Before outlining the project in greater detail, permit me to dwell for a moment upon the different ways of reading the Bible which are implicit in the above rationale/background and incorporated in the retreat material itself. This will make for a more complete understanding of my approach.

Basically, there are three ways in which we can read the Sacred Scriptures. We can read *reflectively*, using the Bible as a resource for prayer; we can read *academically*, using the Bible as an object of study; and we can read *contextually*, using the Bible as a source of moral and spiritual guidance and of prophetic judgment.

This Johannine retreat has been developed in the belief that these three ways are mutually supportive rather than mutually exclusive. The question is not 'What is the best way of reading the text?' but 'What is the appropriate way of reading it at this point in time?'

Introduction 17

We know that Jesus himself, though he would probably not have made such distinctions, read God's Word in the Hebrew Scriptures in these three ways. As with all Jews, the Psalter was his prayerbook. He studied the sacred writings (cf. Lk 2:46-47). He quoted from them in his teaching ministry and interpreted them anew, using well-established rabbinical methods. Moreover, he applied them to his own life-context and to that of his hearers (cf. Lk 24:13-35 — the meeting of the risen Lord with the two disciples en route to Emmaus; and, perhaps less to the point, Mt 4:1-11 and parallels — the temptation of Jesus in the wilderness).

OUTLINE OF THE RETREAT
Representative figures

Depending on the texts chosen for special attention, the way the material is structured and presented, and the specific goals that one has in mind, it would be possible to construct a Johannine retreat in many different (if not logically distinct) ways. The retreat could be based, for example, on the passion narrative or on the supper discourse; or it could pursue throughout the Gospel as a whole one or more of John's distinctive theological themes.

One such theme, which lies at the very heart of the Gospel and which must of necessity colour every attempt to devise a Johannine retreat, is the theme of faith. For this reason, a comprehensive treatment of this theme has been included among the preparatory essays which the participant is exhorted to read in the weeks leading up to the retreat (see later).

The originality of the present retreat lies, I believe, in its structure. My preference in assembling the material has been to direct the retreatant's attention, in the first place, to the *experience* of a wide selection of the *representative figures* in this Gospel of 'pure relationship', always acknowledging, of course, that the focal point of our reflection over the entire six days is Jesus himself.

One advantage of this choice is that it should serve to remind us of the fact that the Good News is not some abstruse doctrine; it is for and about real human beings — the early Christian communities in the first place and the disciples of Jesus, ourselves included, across the ages. It should also prompt us to move beyond a consideration of the various responses of those who encounter Jesus to a serious appraisal of our own faith commitment.

The representative figures we will consider are as follows:

Day 1	Nicodemus	3:1-21,31-36; 7:37-52; 19:38-42
Day 2	the Samaritan woman	4:1-42
Day 3	the man born blind	9:1-41
Day 4	Martha, Mary and Lazarus	11:1-44; 12:1-11,17
Day 5	Peter, Judas and Thomas	*passim*
Day 6	the mother of Jesus and the beloved disciple	2:1-12; 19:25-27; *passim*

Format

The format for each day is the same, although the retreatant is invited (indeed, encouraged) to adapt the material as she or he thinks fit. It is recommended, however, that the following sequence be adhered to even when the time allocations/allotments are changed to suit local circumstances or personal preference:

7.45 - 8.00 a.m.   Breakfast.
8.40 - 10.25 a.m.   Reflective study of the set scripture text(s) with the aid of the detailed commentary provided. A short break may be taken at some convenient time.

Introduction 19

10.55 - 11.35 a.m.	Imaginative prayer based on the experience of the representative figure.
12.10 - 12.40 p.m.	Imaginative prayer based on the experience of Jesus.
1.00 - 1.40 p.m.	Dinner (perhaps with suitable recorded music).
5.00 - 6.00 p.m.	Contextual application of the set scripture text(s).
6.30 - 7.00 p.m.	Supper (perhaps with suitable recorded music).
7.45 - 8.30 p.m.	*Ad libitum* (time for journalling, art work, et cetera).
9.00 - 9.30 p.m.	Centring prayer using a mantra drawn from or based on the day's scripture reading.

To emphasise the different character of each of the above elements, it is recommended that the retreatant choose on a regular daily basis appropriately different locations for the various exercises. Some places will be found more conducive than others to the 'task' at hand.

MODES OF PRAYER

Apart from the meals and the *ad libitum* period, it will be noted that the five elements in the above outline embrace with differing emphases the academic, reflective and contextual approaches to reading the Bible which were outlined above. Each element involves, in a logical progression, complementary modes of prayer which we will now consider in turn.

Reflective study of the set scripture text(s)

I have no hesitation in including, under the heading of prayer, the rather lengthy time spent each morning in studying the chosen texts. Such study, when undertaken with the right dispositions and with a reverent awareness of the presence of God, is indeed, as many Jews believe, an act of worship.

It is one of the ways in which we, as people of faith, can reach out to God, and thereby encounter a God who is reaching out to us and who wishes to communicate with us more lovingly than we can ever comprehend.

To facilitate a deeper understanding of the text and to assist the retreatant to enter, as it were, more fully into the mind and heart of the evangelist, I have prepared detailed commentaries on the passages which relate most directly to the faith journeys of our chosen representative figures.

These commentaries, as the cited passages reveal, are based on extensive reading of standard works and the ever increasing volume of journal articles on the Johannine writings which are not readily available to most of the people for whom this 'do-it-yourself' retreat is primarily intended. Understandably, special attention has been given to the scholarly contributions of contemporary authors.

The commentaries, which are intended to be comprehensive but not exhaustive, are pitched at the level of the intelligent non-specialist reader. For this reason matters of narrowly academic interest are not addressed and a small, but probably adequate, glossary of technical terms is provided. These terms are indicated when they first appear in the text and later, where appropropriate, by means of an asterisk.

In reading these commentaries, the retreatant should not burden himself or herself by looking up all the scriptural references that are given. For the most part they are included for the benefit of readers who may wish to devote additional time to study of the material at some later date. Likewise, there is no obligation on the retreatant, especially if it proves distracting, to consult all the footnotes.

Introduction

Occasionally a more important footnote is indicated in the text by means of a superscript number in bold type.

It might be asked how my commentary material differs from that to be found in standard commentaries on the Fourth Gospel. While readily acknowledging that similarities abound, I would like to think that the overall conception of my project as a resource for a particular type of renewal experience colours not only my choice of texts but also my treatment of them. There is, I believe, a certain coherence in this treatment which derives both from its intended usefulness as an aid to contemplative prayer and from the theme of faith which serves to unify the passages chosen.

Specific suggestions regarding the effective use of the commentaries will be included later.

Imaginative prayer based on the experience of the representative figure

The day's study segment completed, it should now be possible for the participant, after a breathing space, to enter empathetically and with enhanced understanding into the unique faith experience of the representative figure(s) concerned.

The mode of prayer employed here, variously described as 'gospel contemplation' (Sheldrake 1987) and 'imaginative meditation' (Stahl 1977), calls for more than what is commonly understood by devotional reading of the Bible, though it has affinities with the monastic *lectio divina**.

What it entails will be explained more fully in another of the recommended preparatory readings and will be illustrated, at the appropriate place, in the daily materials. For the present it is sufficient to note that, through the exercise of the imagination, the retreatant steps into the milieu of the biblical event(s) which are the subject of the day's reflections by identifying with the representative figure who is the focus of attention.

By entering imaginatively into the world of the 'remembered past', as it is recorded in the inspired Word of God, he or she can expect to confront new challenges and to discover new possibilities in the life of faith in the present.

To pray in this manner is to acknowledge that we have not exhausted the meaning of a text when we have elucidated, by means of diligent study, what the author wished to convey to his original audience. In the light of what the text meant *there and then*, we seek to discover what it may mean *here and now* in the life of the faith community as a whole and in the lives of individual believers.

In this connection, Liebert (1984) has this to say: 'The text necessarily calls into play the consciousness of the interpreter because it is historically structured. Every valid interpretation can therefore be a unique actualisation of the text.'

Imaginative prayer based on the experience of Jesus

Not only is it possible to identify by means of imaginative prayer with the various representative figures whose lives were touched by Jesus, it is also possible (and, I believe, highly desirable) that we should employ similar means to enter into the experience of Jesus himself. Our horarium allocates this third period of prayer to the late morning; but it could be included later in the day if the retreatant finds that arrangement to be more convenient.

This time, rather than identify with Jesus in the unfolding narrative, the retreatant is encouraged to sit with Jesus as he casts his mind back over the events of the day and reflects upon them in the light of his understanding of the mission of salvation that the Father has entrusted to

Introduction

him. It is, therefore, not so much a question of entering into the experience of Jesus as he interacts with the people he meets as of entering into the prayer which this daily commerce occasions. It is rather like being present when Jesus makes what we would call, in today's terminology, his *examination of consciousness**.

This is a privileged moment in our retreat when, having this mind in us which was also in Christ Jesus, we pray with him who constantly makes intercession for us (cf 1 Tim 2:5-6; Heb 8:1-6).

Contextual application of the set scriptural text(s)

Having completed a full morning of study and reflective prayer, the retreatant is advised to relax after dinner for a few hours. This time may be divided between rest and physical exercise. A moderately long walk can be helpful if some suitable place can be found.

In the late afternoon, conscious of the fact that the Christian is addressed by the Gospel as surely as the representative figures were addressed by Jesus, the retreatant is invited to enter more deliberately and more directly into his or her own mind and heart. Some of the fruits of the morning's sowing may now be harvested as the text interprets the interpreter and an attempt is made to relate the scripture to the circumstances of one's own life in the present.

Apropos of these matters, Gula (1984:299) observes:

> Critical approaches to interpreting the Bible affirm that anyone who comes to Scripture as a believing member of the community shaped by the Bible can find some personal meaning from the text that is valid, even though it may not be the meaning intended by the author.

This personal meaning will vary considerably from one retreatant to another for the simple reason that each person brings to the reading of the sacred text his or her own unique life experience. Even for the same reader this meaning will vary from year to year as familiar biblical passages are read again. The text does not change but the reader does; and, as new meanings are discovered, the horizon of personal experience expands and further opportunities for growth in the life of the Spirit are revealed.

It is hoped that, through this contextual reflection on the personal myths* of such people as the man born blind and the Samaritan woman, we will identify the aspects of their story which resonate with our own. More importantly, we will identify, perhaps through our feelings of resistance, those elements which judge us and invite us to conversion.

'Revelation', as Sandra Schneiders (1984:106) observes, 'is most clearly revelation when it breaks through our personal biases and social prejudices and challenges us to change our way of thinking.'

Guidelines and pertinent questions are included in the retreat material to assist the participant in this potentially very fruitful exercise. They are not intended to be prescriptive. Nor do they imply that we read the Christian and Hebrew Scriptures to find quite specific answers to all of life's problems.

Centring prayer using a mantra

The fifth and final time of prayer, provided for in the retreat timetable, involves the use of a mantra. This is a phrase or statement taken from (or based on) the day's scripture reading(s). It may even be a single word. Suggestions are given in the retreat material; but it is preferable that the retreatant himself or herself choose a mantra which, in the light of the foregoing contextual reflection, has special personal significance.

Introduction

Having adopted a comfortable position (more will be said about techniques later), we repeat the mantra rhythmically and in a low voice, synchronising it throughout with our breathing.

Repetitive prayer of one kind or another is common in many religious traditions. Both Moslems and Christians make use of a rosary for this purpose. The Islamic rosary *(subha)* consists of 99 beads on which the believer recites the 99 praises of God.[3] 'The hundredth praise', as Carretto (1982:85) puts it, 'is a secret, and God reveals it to whomsoever asks him.'

As a magnifying glass, appropriately held, gives greater intensity to the sun's rays, so the mantra focuses our attention on a single point. In Morneau's (1982:10) words, '[It] helps us to slow down, to journey deep within, to feel the pulse of our inner life, to live from a deeper source.' Hopefully, too, at the end of much study and reflection, it will bring simplicity and unity to the prayerful experiences of the entire day.

This is not a time for thought or imagination. After a while, the chosen words do not matter greatly. They become rather like the humming of a mother rocking her child to sleep. One retreatant has told me that, mindful of Romans 8:26, she replaces the mantra at some point with just such a sound. Her own breathing then becomes, as it were, the 'breath of God', the Holy Spirit making intercession 'with inexpressible groanings'.

As a variant to merely reciting the mantra, the retreatant might like to put music to it, after the fashion of Jacques Berthier's Taizé chants, and sing it quietly.

---

3 For a list of these 99 praises of God, see Carretto (1982:84-85).

PREPARATORY READING

Reference has been made in the above outline to reading which the retreatant should undertake in preparation for the six-day retreat or the six single days of recollection. In the first place, all who use this material are urged to read the entire Gospel of John in the weeks leading up to the time of retreat. Though any suitable translation could be used, it should be noted that the *New American Bible* (1970, 1986 [revised New Testament]) is quoted throughout the commentaries.

In addition, three pertinent essays have been included to provide useful background reading to the study of the Gospel and to familiarise the retreatant with what, for some people, may be a new approach to praying the scriptures imaginatively. The essays are entitled: 'John: a Different Gospel', 'Faith in the Fourth Gospel', and 'Imagination and Praying the Gospels'.

SPIRITUALITY AND PERSONALITY

In recent years researchers, using the Enneagram and the Myers-Briggs Type Indicator, have demonstrated that there is a relationship between personality types and various spiritualities.[4] Their findings might be summed up in the words of the title chosen by Keating (1987) for his very practical book on the topic: 'who we are is how we pray'. With this truism in mind, I would not be so rash as to suggest that the retreat I have outlined would prove equally suitable for everyone. My modest hope is that some people will find it helpful at some point in their spiritual journey.

To conclude this introductory chapter, I will make a rather broad assessment, in the light of the above-mentioned

---

4 See Michael and Norrisey (1984) for an interesting account of the findings of the 1982 *Prayer and Temperament Project*.

research, of the suitability of my self-directed Johannine retreat for particular personality types. Because of space constraints my treatment of this matter will, of necessity, be brief and perhaps a little over-simplified.

The Enneagram

The Enneagram, which probably originated in the Sufi (Islamic) mystical tradition, distinguishes nine personality types which it categorises in groupings of three according to whether they are 'head-centred' (5, 6, 7), 'heart-centred' (2, 3, 4), or 'gut-centred' (8, 9, 1). No value judgment is implied in these designations; one type is not better or worse than the others. While we operate at different times out of all three of these centres of power (head, heart and gut), our unique giftedness is to be sought in the one which predominates in our life.

Identifying one's Enneagram type (and the corresponding tendency to compulsion which is characteristic of it) is a means of self-enlightenment which points out the path one must follow in the quest of personal freedom and authentic existence. It can also be of considerable assistance in determining the approaches to prayer which are best calculated to foster one's growth in the life of the Spirit.

The Johannine retreat presented in these pages will appeal more to the 'head-centred' types; but some people in other categories, endeavouring to develop (as is desirable) their weaker centres, will also find it useful.[5]

The Myers-Briggs type indicator

Based on the research of Carl Jung, the Myers-Briggs Type Indicator distinguishes sixteen personality types, each of

---

5 Many books are available on the Enneagram for the reader who would wish to pursue this matter in greater detail. See, for example, Bessing, *et al* (1984).

which is identified in terms of four of the eight paired qualities/characteristics which are to be found in varying degrees of emphasis in the human personality. These paired qualities are: Extraverted/Introverted, iNtuitive/Sensing, Feeling/Thinking, Judging/Perceiving. It is the combination of the four qualities which predominate in a given individual which defines that person's personality profile (INFJ in the writer's case).[6]

What was asserted above with reference to the Enneagram applies equally to the MBTI: personality types are neither good nor bad in themselves, only different. They may leave something to be desired, however, if we fail to develop adequately some of our less favoured characteristics, the 'shadow side' of our personality.

Introverts will find themselves more at home with the proposed style of retreat than extraverts. Generally speaking, the former are much less likely to have difficulties with self-direction and with long periods of quiet reflective prayer.

People who are strongly sensate will find the rather structured approach of the retreat to their liking; but they may run into some difficulties in the exercise of the active imagination in those prayer sessions which call upon one to enter into the experience of Jesus and the representative figures of the Gospel. On the contrary, intuitive people are usually at ease with such sessions. For them St John's Gospel, pregnant as it is with symbolism, can have a special appeal. Sensors are more likely to be attracted to the 'hands-on' approach of St Mark's Gospel with its graphic presentation of the activity of Jesus.

The study component and the overall structure of the retreat will, I suspect, appeal more readily to thinking

---

[6] For a comprehensive treatment of how these types can fruitfully pursue their natural inclination in different spiritualities and approaches to prayer, see Keating (1987).

types than to feeling types. Both will doubtless impose on the daily prayer sessions their own distinctive stamp, adapting the material when necessary. Where the former are attracted to rather rational styles of prayer, the latter prefer prayer which engages the heart. The retreat, I believe, caters for both.

Whatever our personality type, 'we [who] do not know how to pray as we ought', must ultimately invoke the assistance of the Holy Spirit who, as Paul assures us, 'comes to the aid of our weakness' (Rom 8:26).

FIRST PREPARATORY READING
JOHN: A DIFFERENT GOSPEL

INTRODUCTORY REMARKS

The purpose of this essay, the first of three recommended preparatory readings, is to assist the retreatant to read the Fourth Gospel and to hear the Good News it proclaims in what we might call the 'key' of John. It will summarise the characteristic features of the Gospel and indicate some of the ways in which it differs from the Gospels of Matthew, Mark, and Luke, paying particular attention to the portrayal of Jesus.

KEY TEXTS FOR THE STUDY OF JOHN

Prudence dictates that we should be slow to scan any book of the Christian Scriptures with a view to singling out verses which capture the essence of the writer's message. However, provided that we read them in the light of the Johannine writings as a whole, we can safely point to certain texts which are of crucial importance for an understanding of the Fourth Gospel.

An obvious example is the verse which indicates the writer's purpose in setting down a selection of the many 'signs' that Jesus did in the presence of his disciples and which probably served as the conclusion of the Gospel before the later addition by a redactor of Chapter 21: 'But these are written that you may [come to] believe that Jesus is the Messiah, the Son of God, and that through this belief you may have life in his name' (20:31; cf. 11:27).

In marked contrast to this statement of purpose are the many references to those who, having heard Jesus' word and witnessed his signs, rejected him. The first of these is in the prologue: 'He came to what was his own, but his own people did not accept him' (1:11). This is surely the most telling example of irony in the Gospel. From among the very people who had waited so patiently through the centuries for the coming of the Messiah, there were some who delivered him over to death when he came among them.

Other key verses define the nature of our Saviour's mission:

> For God so loved the world that he gave his only Son, so that everyone who believes in him might not perish but might have eternal life (3:16).

> 'I came into the world as light, so that everyone who believes in me might not remain in darkness' (12:46).

> 'For this I was born and for this I came into the world, to testify to the truth' (18:37).

> 'I came so that they might have life and have it more abundantly' (10:10).

In this connection we could also point to the seven different 'I am ...' statements of Jesus in which he identifies himself as 'the bread of life' (6:35,41,48), 'the light of the world' (8:12; 9:50); 'the gate for the sheep' (10:7,9); 'the good shepherd' (10:11,14), 'the resurrection and the life' (11:25), 'the true vine' (15:1,5), and 'the way and the truth and the life' (14:6).

John: A different Gospel

Within a retreat context, we might also give heed to those texts which define the role of the faithful disciple,[1] taking to heart such words of Jesus as: 'This is how all will know that you are my disciples, if you have love for one another' (13:35; cf. 15:9-10); and, 'As the Father has sent me, so I send you' (20:21; cf. 17:18).

In addition to these statements, there are some questions on the lips of Jesus which retreatants might listen to as if they were addressed to them personally: 'What are you looking for?' (1:38; cf. 18:4,7; 20:15). 'Do you want to be well?' (5:6). 'Do you believe in the Son of Man?' (9:35). 'I am the resurrection and the life .... Do you believe this?' (11:25-26). 'Do you realise what I have done for you?' (13:12). 'Do you love me?' (21:15,16,17).

JOHANNINE THEMES

One way to identify the principal themes of St John's Gospel (and, therefore, the theological and pastoral preoccupations of its writer) is by doing a word frequency count. Having done this, we may see some relevance in Comblin's (1979:vii) assertion: 'In a sense the entire substance of the Fourth Gospel consists of fifteen words, and Jesus' discourses in the Fourth Gospel concern all the possible connections among these fifteen words.'

The distinctive quality of this Gospel is all the more apparent when we take some of the writer's most frequently used words and compare the number of times they are used in Matthew and Luke. A partial list follows, with acknowledgements to Weber (1981:220):

---

[1] It is interesting to note that John uses the word 'disciples' no fewer than 78 times, whereas he never uses the word 'apostles' and speaks of 'the Twelve' only four times.

Greek key word	English equivalent	Jn	Mt	Lk
agapān, agapē	to love, love	43	9	13
alētheia	truth	25	1	3
doxazein, doxa	to glorify, glory	41	11	22
zēn, zoē	to live, life	53	13	14
Iēsous	Jesus	237	150	89
Ioudaios	Jew	71	5	5
kosmos	the world	78	8	3
martyrein, martyria	to testify, testimony	47	1	2
menein	to remain	40	3	7
patēr (used of God)	the Father	118	45	17
pempein	to send	32	4	10
pisteuein	to believe	98	11	9
phōs	light	23	7	7

Space does not permit any elaboration of these themes here. Their relevance to an in-depth study of John will become abundantly clear as the reader studies the detailed commentaries on the texts chosen for the six days of the retreat. The theme of faith will be the subject of the next preparatory reading.

JOHN AND THE SYNOPTICS*
Significant omissions

John omits from his Gospel much that might have been considered common knowledge among the Christians of his day, especially when such detail is not judged to be germane to his purpose and witness. For example, there is no account in the Fourth Gospel of:

    Jesus' virginal conception and birth
    Jesus' baptism in the Jordan (alluded to)
    Jesus' temptations in the desert
    the transfiguration
    Peter's confession at Caesarea Philippi
    the formal institution of the Blessed Eucharist

the agony in the garden at Gethsemane
the ascension into heaven.

Also notably absent from John are the story parables which are such a feature of the other Gospels. According to Crossan's (1975:47-62) typology of storytelling, parables (stories which overturn a world) stand at the opposite end of the spectrum from myths (stories which create a world). It could be that they have no place in the Fourth Gospel because therein Jesus himself is the 'parable' who turns the world of his day upside down by all that he says and does.

Moreover, while John is alive to the struggle between Jesus and 'the ruler of this world' (12:31; 14:30; 16:11), he has no place for healing miracles which involve demonic possession (contrast Mark 1:23-28; 5:1-10; 7:25-30; 9:17-27).

Significant inclusions

Perhaps even more noteworthy than the omissions listed above is the importance that John attaches to events which are not referred to in the Synoptics: the special call of Nathanael (1:45-51), the marriage feast at Cana (2:1-11), the encounter with the Samaritan woman (4:4-42), Nicodemus's visit to Jesus (3:1-15), the cure of the man born blind (9:1-41), the raising of Lazarus (11:1-44), Jesus' meeting with some Greeks (12:20-36), the washing of the disciples' feet (13:1-20), the supper discourses with their rather fully developed theology of the Holy Spirit (14-17), the special appearance of the resurrected Jesus to Thomas (20:26-30).

We could also point to the special role assigned to the 'beloved disciple' by John and his fuller characterisation of some of the other disciples: Thomas (he speaks only in this Gospel), Andrew, Peter, Philip, and Judas.

He has, moreover, an eye for small details which add vividness and a note of verisimilitude to the narrative. John alone mentions that there are 'six stone water jars' at Cana (2:6), that the loaves which Jesus distributes in a place where there is 'a great deal of grass' (6:10) are 'barley loaves' (6:9), that the disciples have rowed 'about three or four miles' (6:19) when they see Jesus walking on the lake, that it is night when Judas leaves on his mission of betrayal (13:13), that it is beside 'a charcoal fire' that Peter denies Jesus (18:18) and later professes his love for him (21:9), that 'four soldiers' divide Jesus' clothing among them and cast lots for his seamless robe (19:23-24), and that the mixture of myrrh and aloes which Joseph and Nicodemus bring to the tomb weighs 'about one hundred pounds' (19:39).

Just as these small details give the impression that the 'writer' of the Gospel was in fact an eye-witness of the events he narrates, so also does his specialised knowledge of Palestine and Jerusalem point to one who was more than casually associated with the life of Jesus.

He knows of two Bethanies, one of which is beyond the Jordan (cf. 1:28; 12:1). He knows, too, of the Sheep Gate and the nearby pool called Bethesda (5:2); the Pool of Siloam (9:7); the Portico of Solomon (10:23); the Kidron valley (18:1); the 'Stone Pavement, in Hebrew, Gabbatha' (19:13); and 'the Place of the Skull, in Hebrew, Golgotha' (19:17). Our writer is also aware that Bethsaida is the home of three of Jesus' disciples — Philip, Andrew and Peter (1:44; 12:21), that Cana (Nathanael's town) is in Galilee (2:1; 4:46; 21:2), and that Sychar is in Samaria near Jacob's well (4:5).

There is plenty of evidence for his knowledge of Jewish life and history. He notes, for example, how long it took to build the Temple (2:20); and he comments knowingly on the long-standing enmity between the Jews and the Samaritans (4:9), the poor estimation of women in Jewish

John: A different Gospel

society (4:9,27), and Jesus' attitude towards the sabbath regulations (5:10,16-18; 7:21-23; 9:14-16).

In connection with these details, it is well to remember that Jerusalem was destroyed in 70 C.E. and that the Fourth Gospel took its final shape about 30 years later.

Significant differences
Chronology

In this Gospel Jesus begins his preaching ministry while John the Baptist is still actively engaged in his work (cf. 3:22-30; 4:1-2) whereas, in the other canonical* Gospels, his cousin is already in prison by then (cf. Mt 4:12,17; Mk 1:14; Lk 3:18-20).

From a reading of Matthew, Mark, and Luke we can infer that Jesus' ministry occupies hardly more than one year (they mention only one Passover* feast). However, in John it would seem that the ministry of Jesus is spread out over somewhat more than two years. Historically, the Fourth Gospel, which mentions three Passover feasts (2:13,23; 6:4; 11:55) is probably nearer the mark.

In John the 'cleansing' of the Temple (symbolic of the inauguration of a new era) occurs at the beginning of Jesus' ministry (2:13-22). The other evangelists place it towards the end of Jesus' ministry in the sequence of events leading up to his passion and death (Mt 21:12-13 // Mk 11:15-16 // Lk 19:45-46).

Finally, we may note that Jesus' last meal with 'his own' and his death and burial take place before the Passover celebration in John, whereas, in the Synoptic Gospels, the last meal of Jesus with his disciples is in progress at the very time that other Jews are partaking of their Passover meal.[2]

---

[2] A chart in Kysar (1975:5) will help to clarify this matter (note that the Jewish day began at sundown).

Scene of Jesus' ministry

In the Synoptic Gospels Jesus' ministry is exercised in Galilee; he reaches Jerusalem (in Judaea) only in the last week of his life. John's focus is quite different. He presents Jesus as working mainly in Judaea, recording five visits of Jesus to Jerusalem (2:13; 5:1; 7:10; 10:22-23; 12:12) compared with one in Mark's Gospel (Mk 14:12ff.). Jesus does occasionally minister in Galilee (2:1-3 — Cana wedding feast; 4:46-54 — cure of the royal official's son) or retire there for reasons of personal safety (4:1-3 — via Samaria; cf. 7:1).

Vocabulary

We have already noted, when speaking about Johannine themes, some of the words which John uses more frequently than the other evangelists (life, light, truth, world, Father, et cetera). Equally notable is the rarity or absence of certain terms to be found in the Synoptic Gospels (kingdom, demons, power, pity, gospel, preach, parable, repent, tax-collector, Sadducees, apostles, et cetera).

Scholars have also pointed to as many as 50 expressions which John favours and which are not found in the Synoptic writings, for example: the last day (6:39,40,44,54; 11:24; 12:48; cf. 7:37); and 'to lay down one's life' (10:15, 17,18; 13:37,38; 15:13; 1 Jn 3:16).[3]

JOHANNINE CHRISTOLOGY

Christology is that area of theological reflection which has as its focus the person, mission and ministry of Jesus

---

[3] John also uses several transliterated Aramaic* words which he usually explains for the benefit of his non-Semitic readers, for example: Kephas (1:42), Thomas (11:16; 20:24), Messiah (4:25), Rabbouni (20:16), Siloam (9:7), Gabbatha (19:13), and Golgotha (19:17).

Christ. Scholars commonly distinguish two approaches to this study: a *descending* approach which begins 'from above' with the heavenly Word of God *(Logos)* and an *ascending* approach which begins 'from below' with the historical Jesus. It is probably not an oversimplification to suggest that the emphasis in the Johannine and Pauline writings is on the former approach and in the Synoptics on the latter.

However, even a cursory reading of the four Gospels would indicate that each of the evangelists has provided us with his own distinctive profile of Jesus, highlighting and theologically elaborating different aspects of our Saviour's ministry.

The writing of 'John the theologian', as he was called in early Christian times, is rather more contemplative in tone. For some readers the lineaments of his portrait of Jesus may not be as obvious at first glance as those of the Synoptics' portraits of the God-man. As McPolin (1979:256) says, they may 'elude us behind long, abstract discourses and the seeming lack of actions and interaction'.

There is nonetheless, to quote McPolin (1979:257) again, 'a wholeness about Johannine Christology not matched by any other New Testament writing'. We acknowledge that the incarnate Word of the Fourth Gospel is possessed of supernatural knowledge and power (1:47-48; 2:24-25; 4:16-18; 6:5-6; *inter alia*) and is serenely in control of every situation; but we must never lose sight of the fact that 'Jesus, son of Joseph, from Nazareth' (1:45; cf. 6:42) is as unmistakably human as the Gospel's author.

He may not emerge from the pages of John as the vividly human and limited Jesus of Mark; but the contours of the Lucan portrait of a man of great compassion are surely in evidence. That he loves people deeply is frequently demonstrated and is expressly stated in a number of places (11:3,5,36; 13:1,23,34; 15:9,12-13; 19:26; 20:2; 21:7,20). Moreover, like any human being, he entertains the hope of being loved in return (14:15; 21:15-17). He exhorts his disciples to remain in his love just as he remains in the love of his Father (15:9-10).

The passion narrative

It is in the narrative of Jesus' passion and death that the distinctive features of Johannine Christology are most clearly revealed. For John the passion of Jesus is the moment of triumph to which his whole life has led. It is the hour that Jesus spoke of at Cana (2:4; cf. 7:30; 8:20; 12:23,27; 13:1; 17:1), that *kairos** moment when, 'lifted up' on the cross (cf. 3:14; 8:28; 12:32,34), he is uplifted into the glory of his Father.[4]

John stresses the absolutely voluntary character of Jesus' sufferings and death. He has Jesus say in the good shepherd discourse: 'I lay down my life in order to take it up again. No one takes it from me, but I lay it down on my own. I have power to lay it down and power to take it up again' (10:17-18). Therefore, there is no need for the betrayer's kiss in this Gospel. Jesus boldly steps forward in the garden and asks the Roman soldiers, 'Whom are you looking for?' (18:4,7). They fall to the ground when, identifying himself as 'Jesus the Nazorean', he utters the divine name — I AM (18:5,8).

Nor is there any need for Simon the Cyrenian (cf. Mt 27:32 // Mk 15:21 // Lk 23:26) to assist Jesus with his heavy and shameful burden. 'So they took Jesus', writes John, 'and carrying the cross himself he went out to what is

---

[4] We find the word 'glory' 38 times in John. It is expressive of the mysterious presence and saving power of the God of covenant love made manifest historically in the life of Jesus. Commentators commonly divide the Gospel into the Book of Signs (1-12) and the Book of Glory (13-21).

called the Place of the Skull, in Hebrew, Golgotha' (19:16-17).

There is no heart-rending cry of anguish from the cross in the Fourth Gospel (cf. Mt 27:46 // Mk 15:34); and we are not told that Jesus cries out 'in a loud voice' as he yields up his spirit (cf. Mt 27:50 // Mk 15:37 // Lk 23:46). Jesus' final words on the cross in John are a triumphant 'It is finished' (19:30).

Not surprisingly, then, though John exploits the symbolic values of light and darkness elsewhere in his Gospel, he does not mention the darkness which, as the other evangelists tell us, descends upon Calvary for three hours while Jesus hangs upon the cross (Mt 27:45 // Mk 15:33 // Lk 23:44). This is the moment when the one who '[has come] into the world as light' (12:46; cf. 8:12; 9:4; 1 Jn 1:5-7) overcomes the powers of darkness (cf. 1:5).

Similarly appropriate is the fact that John makes no reference to the rending of the Temple curtain at the time of Jesus' death. It is superfluous in view of Jesus' declaration of himself as the new Temple, the privileged place of God's presence to his people, on the occasion of his expulsion of the money-changers from the holy precincts (2:13-21).[5]

LITERARY FEATURES/TECHNIQUES

Though the literary features of the Fourth Gospel have little direct relevance to our prayerful reflection on the sacred text, a brief consideration of some of the more important of them will help to underscore the distinctiveness

---

[5] John records this dramatic event at the beginning of Jesus' public life. In the Synoptic Gospels, on the other hand, it occurs after Jesus' triumphal entry into Jerusalem (Mt 21:12-13 // Mk 11:15-17 // Lk 19:45-46), setting in train the events which lead to his passion.

of the Johannine writings and make the commentaries on the chosen texts easier to follow.

Irony

Of special interest is John's use of irony — a dramatic device whereby a character's unawareness of the difference between appearance and reality puts him or her at a considerable disadvantage, often with comic effect. Though it shares with metaphor the element of disparity between literal statement and intended meaning, it seeks to do far more than explicate the truth by means of a striking comparison.

The purpose of irony in this Gospel is to call established positions and cherished assumptions (our own included) into question and to reveal truth by challenging and exposing the shortcomings of those to whom Jesus says: 'Stop judging by appearances, but judge justly' (7:24).

When we come to identify the victims of the Gospel's ironies, we must include almost everyone.[6] 'The Jews' head the list, especially their religious leaders who are representative figures of those in whose disbelief there is (as they are portrayed by the evangelist)[7] an element of wilfulness, even of perversity. The rejection of Jesus by some people from amongst those who had waited for centuries for the coming of the Messiah (cf. 1:10), which is the basis of most of the ironies in the Fourth Gospel, culminates in the very sin of blasphemy of which Jesus himself is accused: 'We have no king but Caesar' (19:15).

---

6 The list would include: Nathanael (1:46), the headwaiter at Cana (2:9-10), Nicodemus (3:2), the Samaritan woman (4:12), Thomas (11:16), and Pilate (18:38).

7 Later, when we consider the story of the man born blind, we will note the reasons for John's negative approach to the Jewish leaders. It needs to be stressed repeatedly that his perspective, conditioned as it was by historical factors, is not to be taken as normative for later generations of Christians.

Often in John, the ignorance of people is made manifest with ironic effect by means of an unanswered question and, one might add, by the untenable assumption which underlies it (cf. 1:46; 4:12; 8:22,53; 9:40; 18:38) or by their confident assertion of erroneous or limited points of view (cf. 6:42; 7:52; 9:16; 13:37-38; 14:8-9). In addition, they occasionally speak truths the profundity of which escapes them but not the readers of the Gospel (cf. 12:19; 19:14). The prime example of this is the statement of Caiaphas: 'You know nothing, nor do you consider that it is better for you that one man should die instead of the people, so that the whole nation may not perish' (11:50). Of course, as John's readers knew, the Temple and the nation suffered the fate which the Jewish leaders had hoped to forestall.

Misunderstanding

Just as in the Synoptic Gospels Jesus' hearers frequently misunderstand his parables, so also in John's Gospel they misunderstand the figures of speech he employs. They take the literal meaning instead of the figurative. Whilst these misunderstandings, which are sometimes linked with irony, are usually in character or at least contribute to the characterisation, they are essentially a dramatic technique which sets the scene for the protagonist to give a clarifying discourse or for the evangelist to provide explanatory comment.

Frequently it is the crowd or 'the Jews' who fail to comprehend Jesus' meaning (cf. 2:19-21; 6:32-35,51-53; 7:33-36; 8:21-22,31-35,51-53,56-58; 12:32-34). One of their number, the learned Nicodemus, misunderstands Jesus' words about being 'born from above' (3:3-5). He fares no better (in fact, distinctly worse) than an unlettered Samaritan woman (4:10-15).

Even Jesus' own followers have difficulty in grasping the full import of what he has to say to them (cf. 4:31-34; 11:11-15,23-25; 13:36-38; 14:4-6,7-9; 16:16-19).

Concerning the writer's frequent and distinctive use of the misunderstanding technique, Painter (1979:82) remarks:

> The misunderstanding motif is historically based, dramatically developed and has a pedagogical purpose in the structure of the Gospel. John wrote to remove inadequate attitudes to Jesus which would not be able to stand the test of Jewish persecution.

Implied in this statement are other functions which we could label pastoral and apologetic* and which are especially in evidence in the misunderstandings which relate to the theological issues surrounding Jesus' death, resurrection and glorification.

Dialogue becoming monologue

Several times John presents a narrative which leads into a dialogue between Jesus and his questioners who imperceptibly disappear from the scene, leaving Jesus to deliver a monologue of more universal interest. Read again the story of the meeting between Jesus and Nicodemus (3:1-21). Where is the Pharisee after 3:10?

Similarly in the supper discourses (13-17) various speakers recede into the background and Jesus' words take the form of a monologue.

Lengthy discourses

The Johannine Jesus does not speak in parables drawn from rural life and only occasionally makes use of the kind of aphoristic statements we find more commonly in the other Gospels (cf. Mt 9:12 // Mk 2:17 // Lk 5:31; Lk 4:23).[8]

---

8 For further information on Jesus' use of proverbs and rabbinic aphorisms, see Collins (1986).

John: A different Gospel

He delivers extended discourses which are often complex and sometimes rather abstract. These discourses reflect the homiletic tradition of the writer's faith community and the action of the Spirit therein (cf. 15:26-27; 16:13-14).

In some Bibles the discourse passages are printed in verse form. This does not imply that they were originally poems or hymns; but it does highlight their lyrical quality and may, I believe, assist memorisation.

The five discourses in Matthew's Gospel take the form of thematic monologues. In John, on the other hand, the discourses are much more frequent and take a variety of forms: dialogue, monologue, or a mixture of both dialogue and monologue. They are commonly associated with some narrative material which tends to be of secondary interest compared with Jesus' words. Typical Johannine discourses can be found in: 3:1-21; 4:4-38; 5:1-47; 6:22-58; 9:39-10:21; 10:22-39; 13:31-16:33.

DRAMATIC TECHNIQUES

'One of the most striking characteristics of the Fourth Gospel', observes Flanagan (1981:264), 'is the way it lends itself to instant theatre.' Not surprisingly, then, in his Collegeville Bible Commentary on the Johannine writings (1983:46-7,92-3), he sets out the account of the cure of the man born blind (9:1-41) and the whole of chapter 20 as 'scripts' for plays. With equal reason he might have chosen chapters 4 (the Samaritan woman) and 11 (the raising of Lazarus).

As there is an obvious overlap between the literary and dramatic features of the Gospel, we have already commented on some of John's preferred dramatic techniques. Amongst others that he employs, we might note the following.

The rule of two

Storytellers often limit dialogue to two people (or groups of people) at a time. Good examples of this technique are to be found in the two narratives just referred to: the Samaritan woman (4:4-42) and the raising of Lazarus (11:1-44).

It is linked with the *double-stage technique* in the trial of Jesus before Pilate, the seven scenes of which alternate between inside and outside the Praetorium (18:28-19:16).

Foreshadowing

Part of the stock-in-trade of every good storyteller is the ability to create suspense or a sense of anticipation by revealing a glimpse of future events. This is used quite effectively in this Gospel in: 1:11; 11:4; 11:49-50; 12:32-33; 13:36; 16:32; 21:18.

'Stage-props'

Even apparently inconsequential details can have a certain dramatic suggestiveness for the alert reader or listener. Flanagan (1981:266) sees the abandoned water pitcher in 4:28 as 'a stage whisper that the Samaritan woman will return'. Similarly the evangelist uses the 'stage-prop' of a charcoal fire to good dramatic effect in the accounts of Peter's denial of Jesus (18:18) and of his reconciliation with the risen Lord (21:9).

CONCLUDING REMARKS

Our treatment of the characteristic and distinctive features of the Johannine writings has been comprehensive but by no means exhaustive. Other pertinent material will be introduced in the retreat commentaries and in the second of our preparatory essays in which we will consider the very important theme of faith in the Fourth Gospel. All of this, as was stated in the introduction to this book, is intended to help us to listen to the 'spiritual Gospel' in the 'key' of John.

SECOND PREPARATORY READING
FAITH IN THE FOURTH GOSPEL

INTRODUCTION

Both in the narrative sections of the Fourth Gospel and in the discourses, the evangelist develops a number of interrelated themes which clearly reveal his theological preoccupations and his pastoral priorities. Some of these themes are explored by the Synoptic* writers also; but John brings to his writing emphases, nuances and insights which are distinctively his own.

To identify these themes we have only to study, with the help of a concordance*, the vocabulary that the author employs. Such an exercise soon reveals that John's writing is characterised by its repetitiveness, so much so that Comblin (1979:vii) can confidently assert that 'in a sense the entire substance of the Fourth Gospel consists of fifteen words'.

As a further preparation for our retreat reflections on some of the representative figures of the Gospel, we will consider in detail a theme which lies at the very heart of the Johannine presentation of the Good News, namely the theme of faith.

FAITH AS A KEY THEME IN THE FOURTH GOSPEL

From beginning to end, faith is one of the major pastoral and theological concerns of John's Gospel. The text is introduced with a resounding confession of his community's faith: 'In the beginning was the Word, and the Word was with God, and the Word was God' (1:1); and it concludes with a solemn statement of the evangelist's intention to nurture faith in that community. Speaking of the signs that Jesus did in the presence of his disciples, he says: 'But these are written *that you may [come to] believe* that Jesus is the Messiah, the Son of God, and that through this belief you may have life in his name' (20:31).

The first character we meet in the Gospel is John the Baptist. A rather different figure from the Baptist who emerges from the pages of the Synoptic Gospels, he is a man 'sent from God' (1:6; cf. 1:28) whose role, as we are repeatedly reminded, is to bear witness to Jesus. 'He came for testimony, to testify to the light, *so that all might believe through him*' (1:7; cf. 1:8,15,19,32,34; 3:26,28; 5:33-36). His most direct testimony to Jesus is to be found in a passage which has been incorporated in some Eucharistic liturgies: 'Behold, the Lamb of God, who takes away the sin of the world' (1:29; cf. 1:36).

We find other titles indicative of faith on the lips of Jesus' disciples. Andrew testifies to his brother Simon that Jesus is 'the Messiah' (1:41). Philip invites Nathanael to meet 'the one whom Moses wrote about in the law*, and also the prophets' (1:45). Incredulous at first, Nathanael, having met Jesus of Nazareth, says to him, 'Rabbi, you are the Son of God; you are the King of Israel' (1:49). Later, after the miracle of the loaves and fishes, Peter, speaking on behalf of the other true followers of Jesus, confesses, 'We have come to believe and are convinced that you are the Holy One of God' (6:69).

At the empty tomb, where the beloved disciple 'saw and believed' (20:8; cf. 21:7), Mary Magdalen encounters the risen Jesus and hastens to announce to the disciples, 'I have seen the Lord' (20:18). Her words find their echo in what they proclaim to Thomas (20:25) who himself comes to acknowledge Jesus in a confession of faith which climaxes all such utterances in the Fourth Gospel, 'My Lord and my God!' (20:28).

Elsewhere in John the faith of the disciples collectively is affirmed. After 'the beginning of [Jesus'] signs in Cana in Galilee', for example, we are told that 'his disciples began to believe in him' (2:11; cf. 2:22; 16:27; 17:8); and during the supper discourse they say to Jesus, 'Now we realise that you know everything .... Because of this we believe that you came from God' (16:30).

In addition to the above, we could point to the faith witness of the family at Bethany. Both Martha and Mary state that Lazarus would not have died if Jesus had been present (11:21,32); and Martha, even before the raising of her brother, says to Jesus, 'Yes, Lord. I have come to believe that you are the Messiah, the Son of God, the one who is coming into the world' (11:27; cf. 20:31).

We have also the example of the Samaritan woman and her townspeople for whom Jesus is 'truly the savior of the world' (4:42); of the royal official who together with 'his whole household came to believe' (4:53); and of the man born blind who worships at Jesus' feet saying, 'I do believe, Lord' (9:38).

Furthermore, and speaking more generally, the evangelist notes that 'many of the crowd began to believe in him', and said, 'When the Messiah comes, will he perform more signs than this man has done?' (7:31; cf. 2:23; 4:39,41; 7:31; 8:30; 10:42; 11:45; 12:11). These included 'many, even among the authorities' (12:42), most notably Joseph of Arimathea who was 'secretly a disciple of Jesus for fear of the Jews' (19:38).

In the light of the above, one could hardly dispute the observation of de la Croix (1966:219) that 'Christ cannot appear in [John's] Gospel without the problem of faith immediately coming up'. There is hardly a character of any significance in the Gospel who does not affirm or deny his or her faith in Jesus.

WHAT IS FAITH FOR JOHN?

It should be obvious (but it needs to be stated nonetheless) that, for the writer of the Fourth Gospel, faith involves much more than speculative knowledge about God and more than mere intellectual recognition of Jesus as Saviour. Faith in the Johannine sense of the term is not simply adherence to a body of revealed truth but adherence to the revealer of the truth, to the one who is himself the Truth (14:6; cf. 1 Jn 5:20).

Faith calls for the acceptance of what is said authoritatively about Jesus in the inspired Word of God and for the reception of the self-revelation of Jesus recorded therein; but the ultimate object of our faith must ever be Jesus himself, the Word made flesh (1:14), and the Father who sent him into the world (14:1). 'Whoever believes in me believes not only in me', says Jesus, 'but also in the one who sent me, and whoever sees me sees the one who sent me' (12:44-45; cf. 14:9).

To deny Jesus, therefore, is also to deny the Father, as John points out so forcibly in his first epistle:

> Who is the liar? Whoever denies that Jesus is the Christ. Whoever denies the Father and the Son, this is the antichrist. No one who denies the Son has the Father, but whoever confesses the Son has the Father as well (1 Jn 2:22-23; cf. 5:10-12; Jn 5:23).

Christian faith finds expression in an intimate relationship with God (cf. 1 Jn 1:3) in and through the events of daily life which constitute our personal history. 'It appears', in de la Croix's (1966:224) words, 'as the encounter of two persons, drawing one towards the other in a fullness of presence and a totality of surrender'.

FAITH IS A VERB

It is interesting to note that, although faith is one of the most important of the Johannine themes, the evangelist never uses the noun (*pistis* in Greek) in his Gospel and but once only in his three letters (1 Jn 5:4). This is the more notable in view of the fact that it is to be found 244 times in the New Testament.

John's preference is for the verb (*pisteuein* = *'to believe'*) which he employs nine times in his three epistles and 98 times in his Gospel (mostly in Jesus' discourses). By contrast, Matthew, Mark and Luke use this verb only 11 times, 14 times and nine times respectively.

This is fully consonant with what was stated above, namely that, for John, faith is to be understood not primarily as an inner disposition but as an active commitment of oneself to Jesus as the definitive revealer and unique mediator of God's salvation. In Kysar's (1976:81) words: 'Faith is not something one *has*. Faith is something one *does*. Faith is not a static being but a dynamic becoming.'

Pisteuein is used in the Gospel in a number of ways. In some contexts it involves acceptance of the truth of what Jesus has to say (see 2:22; 4:21; 4:50; 5:46-47; 8:45-46; 10:37-38; 14:11). If people find this difficult, Jesus recommends them to look to the congruence between his words and the works he performs in accordance with his Father's will. 'If I do not perform my Father's works, do not believe me; but if I perform them, even if you do not believe me, believe the works, so that you may realise [and understand] that the Father is in me and I am in the Father' (10:37-38; cf. 14:11).

In other contexts the evangelist highlights the need to 'believe *in* [or *into*]' Jesus (3:16; 4:39; 8:30-31; 12:44; 14:1; 17:20) and in the one who sent him (5:24; 11:42; 12:44; 17:8,21). This construction, which occurs three times as often in John as in the rest of the New Testament put together, is expressive not only of simple credence but also of personal commitment. It is the terminology we use to confess our faith when we recite (usually in liturgical settings) one of the traditional Christian creeds.

To believe in Jesus is to follow him, to witness to him, to become not just his admirer but his disciple. In this way, as John assures us in a verse which encapsulates the Good News, we will enjoy eternal life. 'For God so loved the world that he gave his only Son, so that everyone who believes in him might not perish but might have eternal life' (3:16).

Frequently the writer uses the verb 'to believe' absolutely (that is, without a stated object). In most of these instances the object of faith is implied by the context; but, even where this is not so, it is obvious that Jesus Christ, the plenipotentiary of the Father, is the focal point of belief (cf. 4:42; 9:38; 20:29). A simple example is to be found in Jesus' words to the disciples before they leave for Bethany: 'Lazarus has died. And I am glad for you that I was not there, that you may believe' (11:15).

HOW FAITH ARISES

The first thing that needs to be stated is that faith in Jesus as the Christ, the Son of God (cf. 20:31), is the Father's gift before it is our response. 'No one can come to me', says Jesus, 'unless the Father who sent me draw him' (6:44; cf. 10:29). He it is who gives to all who believe in Jesus' name (cf. 1:12; 2:23; 3:18; 20:31) the 'power to become children of God' (1:12).

Faith in the Fourth Gospel

From the Father we receive, at Jesus' request, the gift of the empowering Spirit of truth, the Advocate, who testifies on Jesus' behalf (15:26; cf. 14:16-17,26; 16:13).

That being said, we can add that the beginnings of faith may arise from our openness to searchers like ourselves who witness to Jesus. This is how the neighbours of the Samaritan woman make their first steps towards mature faith (4:28-29; see also 1:35-51). 'Many of the Samaritans of that town began to believe in him because of the word of the woman who testified' (4:39).

However, faith comes more surely from listening to Jesus himself. Not surprisingly, therefore, the Samaritans say to the woman, after enjoying Jesus' company for two days, 'We no longer believe because of your word; for we have heard for ourselves and we know that this is truly the savior of the world' (4:42).

Thomas is not disposed to accept the witness of his fellow disciples at all (20:24-25). It is only when the risen Christ confronts him and admonishes him, 'Do not be unbelieving, but believe', that Thomas makes his profound act of faith, 'My Lord and my God!' (20:27-28).

Implicit in the stories of these and other representative figures in the Fourth Gospel is the need to hear the words of Jesus and to take them to heart. On trial for his life before Pilate, Jesus spells this out very directly when he says, 'Everyone who belongs to the truth listens to my voice' (18:37).

In this statement, as in many texts in the Gospel, there is probably an echo of the evangelist's pastoral concern for those in his own community who were finding the practice of their faith difficult, especially in the face of harassment. He was aware that, even among Jesus' early followers there were those who said to him; 'This saying is hard; who can accept it?' (6:60).

If Jesus' words are fruitful in provoking a response in faith, so also are the wonderful deeds (or 'signs' as John calls them) that he performs. We are told that, during the first of the three Passover* feasts referred to in the Gospel, 'many began to believe in his name when they saw the signs he was doing' (2:23; cf. 2:11; 3:2; 6:2,14; 7:31; 9:16; 10:41-42; 11:45,47-48; 12:18-19,37,42; 20:30-31).

THE INADEQUACY OF SIGNS-FAITH

Jesus expresses his reservations and misgivings about faith based on his miraculous deeds. He remarks rather bluntly to the royal official from Capernaum, 'Unless you people see signs and wonders, you will not believe' (4:48); and he assures Thomas that those 'who have not seen and have believed' are to be accounted 'blessed' (20:29; cf. 6:36).

Faith based on signs has its limitations; it is incomplete. However, it would be extreme to suggest that it is not faith at all, that the first steps of a journey are not part of the journey. Speaking to the Jews in the Portico of Solomon during the Feast of the Dedication*, Jesus replies to their accusation of blasphemy by saying, 'If I do not perform my Father's works, do not believe me; but if I perform them, even if you do not believe me, believe the works...' (10:37-38). And to his disciples, during the first supper discourse, Jesus says, 'Believe me that I am in the Father and the Father is in me, or else, believe because of the works themselves' (14:11).

What Jesus repudiates is any self-seeking in the name of faith. On the day after the miracle of the loaves and fishes (6:1-15), he chides the people who have followed him across the lake to Capernaum in these words, 'Amen, amen, I say to you, you are looking for me not because you saw signs but because you ate the loaves and were filled' (6:26). To follow Jesus it is not enough to see him as a source of here and now advantages; we must perceive his true identity and respond accordingly.

The lesson is clear. Those who aspire to be true disciples of the Lord must be open to the discovery of the spiritual realities signified by his deeds; they must both see and *understand* his signs. What is important for the evangelist and his community is not just that Jesus can restore sight, but that he is the light of the world; not just that he can feed the hungry with bread, but that he himself is the bread of life which alone can satisfy a human being's deepest hunger; not just that he is able to provide water to quench somebody's thirst, but that he is the source of living water 'welling up to eternal life' (4:14); not just that it lies in his power to restore earthly life to the dead, but that he is the resurrection and the life that endures beyond death. For the believer, Jesus not only knows the way to the Father of us all, but is the way. Not only does he teach the truth; he is the Truth incarnate.

One difficulty with basing one's faith on miracles is that sign-events, like so many of our human experiences, are ambiguous; they admit of a variety of interpretations. We can have the experience but miss the meaning, as Eliot says. For some of Jesus' contemporaries, his signs lead not to faith but to animosity. In the Synoptic Gospels (Mt 12:24 // Mk 3:22 // Lk 11:15; cf. Jn 8:48) his power over the evil spirits is attributed to demonic possession; and in John the raising of Lazarus prompts the Pharisees to convene the Sanhedrin to address the question, 'What are we going to do? This man is performing so many signs?' (11:47). With good reason does the evangelist observe, 'Although he had performed so many signs in their presence they did not believe in him ...' (12:37).

Jesus' miracles are conducive to faith only in people who are disposed to see them as possible manifestations of God's saving presence in human history. As Kysar (1976:71) expresses it: 'the signs *require* faith as well as *provoke* faith'.

BELIEVING AND KNOWING

The Johannine theology of faith is not exhausted by a study of the many texts in which John uses the verb *pisteuein*. We need to identify several other words which appear to be synonymous with it in the mind of the writer. For example, as Hermisson and Lohse (1981:164) state: 'Knowing and believing are frequently mentioned together in the Fourth Gospel, and when this is done there is no distinction made between the object of knowledge and that of faith.'

The Samaritans say, 'We know that this is truly the savior of the world' (4:42). 'Know' in this context is interchangeable with 'believe'. The same can be said with reference to Jesus' assurance to his disciples, 'On that day you will realise that I am in my Father and you are in me and I in you' (14:20).

His prayer for them at the last supper furnishes us with another example:

> I pray not only for them, but also for those who will believe in me through their word, ... *that the world may believe* that you sent me. And I have given them the glory you gave me, ... *that the world may know* that you sent me (17:20-23; cf. 16:27-30).

The two terms can be synonymous for John because, though he writes in Greek, he speaks of 'knowing' in the Hebrew sense. In the Hellenistic concept, knowledge proceeds from the detached contemplation of an object in its unchanging essence; but, in the Hebrew mentality, to know is to experience the reality not simply by contemplating it but by entering into it. Like believing, knowing, in biblical thought, involves more than mere intellectual comprehension; it bespeaks a vital personal relationship.

John sometimes defines this relationship in terms of our 'remaining' (Gk *menein*), or 'abiding' in some translations, in the object loved. Especially pertinent to our present discussion of knowing and believing is this text from the first epistle of John: 'We have come to know and to believe in the love God has for us. God is love and whoever remains in love remains in God and God in him' (1 Jn 4:16; cf. 4:15; Jn 14:23; 15:3-10).

This intimate union is assured for those who model their life on the righteous one, Jesus Christ, by keeping his commandments (1 Jn 2:3). 'Whoever claims to abide in him ought to live [just] as he did' (1 Jn 2:6; cf. Jn 15:10).

BELIEVING AND SEEING

Verbs of seeing in this Gospel are also worthy of our close attention; for John makes frequent reference to the relationship between physical sight and spiritual insight, or seeing with the eyes of faith. This is especially pertinent to reflection upon the story of the man born blind (9:1-41) and the postresurrection appearances of Jesus.

To see Jesus in the flesh is one thing; to perceive his true identity is another. Therefore, the request of the Greeks who say to Philip, 'Sir, we would like to see Jesus' (12:21) cannot be met, in its deepest sense, until they are born anew of water and Spirit (cf. 3:3,5) and the risen Jesus is present to them as their Lord and God. Following her encounter with Jesus at the empty tomb, Mary Magdalen announces to the disciples, 'I have *seen* the Lord' (20:18; cf. 20:25). Here, surely, the verb carries a double burden of meaning; for her words are as much a profession of faith as a factual report of her experience. Like the beloved disciple, she 'saw and believed' (20:8).

To illustrate how these two interdependent ways of seeing are related, Kysar (1976:74) uses a nice comparison. 'Maybe the distinction between physical perception and appreciative perception in the art gallery is parallel to the distinction that the evangelist seems to make between physical perception and faith perception.'

BELIEVING AND HEARING

A similar parallel could be drawn between believing and hearing. Because Christian faith calls for obedience (from the Latin *ob* + *audire* = *to hear*) to the truth in perseveringly loving practice, to believe becomes almost synonymous with attentiveness to the words of Jesus. The two go together, as in this text: 'Amen, amen, I say to you, whoever hears my word and believes in the one who sent me has eternal life and will not come to condemnation, but has passed from death to life' (5:24; cf. 8:51; 12:47-50).

Just as we may speak of an inward seeing with the eyes of faith, so also we may speak of an inward hearing with the ears of faith on the part of those who are attuned to their shepherd's voice and follow him (10:27). To such as these Jesus says, 'If you remain in my word, you will truly be my disciples, and you will know the truth, and the truth will set you free' (8:31-32).

On the other hand, there is a deafness, not physical in origin, which afflicts those who 'do not belong to God' (8:47) and whose ears remain perversely closed to the saving truth. Jesus admonishes them, 'Why do you not understand what I am saying? Because you cannot bear to hear my word' (8:43; cf. 8:37).

FAITH AND DISCIPLESHIP

In speaking about the disciples, as we have already noted, the evangelist makes frequent reference to their faith (2:11; 6:67-69; 11:15; 13:19; 14:1,10-12,29; 16:27,30-31; 17:8; 20:8,18,25-29). This is hardly surprising because these two concepts also belong together. With good reason does Brown (1966:512) state: 'For John, being a believer and being a disciple are really synonymous, for faith is the primary factor in becoming a Christian.'

Jesus' disciples are to follow him in loving service, witnessing to him if need be even by their death (cf. 21:18; 12:25-26). In this endeavour both they and those who come after them are supported by his prayer. 'I pray not only for them,' Jesus says to his Father, 'but also for those who will believe in me through their word' (17:20; cf. 17:9).

FAITH AND LOVE

Love is treated in relation to faith in the very first passage in the Gospel which refers to love. Faith is our response in love to God's gift of love in Christ Jesus (3:16; 1 Jn 4:9,14-16). Indeed, as Schnackenburg (1968:559) points out: 'Faith and love sum up for John all the demands imposed on the disciple of Christ.'

Love is Jesus' own criterion of discipleship. To those assembled in the upper room he says, 'I give you a new commandment: love one another. As I have loved you, so you also should love one another. This is how all will know that you are my disciples, if you have love one for another' (13:34-35; cf. 15:12). Such love can truly reflect the love of Jesus only if it is love 'to the end' (13:1; cf. 1 Jn 3:16). 'No one has greater love than this,' he instructs them, 'to lay down one's life for one's friends' (15:13; cf. 1 Jn 3:16).

Before they leave the table of sacred fellowship for the last time, Jesus makes it abundantly clear that he too must be the object of their love (14:15,21,23,24,28; cf. 8:42). It is interesting to note that only in the Fourth Gospel does Jesus speak in such terms.

In this connection, one might reread the last chapter of the Gospel in which Jesus commissions the repentant

Peter only after the disciple has professed his love for him (21:15-17).

The love in question is, like faith, God's gift to us. What can we offer to God that is truly our own except our consent to be loved? 'In this is love: not that we have loved God, but that he loved us and sent his Son as expiation for our sins' (1 Jn 4:10; cf. 3:1).

THE FRUITS OF FAITH

When Jesus assures his disciples that 'whoever believes in the Son has eternal life' (3:36; cf. 5:24; 6:47), he uses the present tense. In the Johannine perspective, eternal life consists in knowing 'the only true God, and the one whom [he] sent, Jesus Christ' (17:3). It is a present possession for the believer; for he or she has even now 'passed from death to life' (cf. 5:24 cf. 1 Jn 3:14).

Death may separate us, the 'children of light' (12:36; cf. 8:12), from our earthly life, but not from God. We have Jesus' word for that. 'I am the resurrection and the life,' he says; 'whoever believes in me, even if he dies, will live, and whoever lives and believes in me will never die' (11:25-26).

Conversely, those who reject Jesus experience judgment rather than liberation (3:18). To those people plotting to kill him, Jesus says, 'If you do not believe that I AM, you will die in your sins' (8:24). These are they who 'remain in darkness' (12:46).

John's approach is more forthright than that of the Synoptic writers. Whereas they frequently point to the necessity of faith in connection with Jesus' miracles of bodily healing (see, among other references, Mt 9:22 // Mk 5:34 // Lk 8:48), John sees faith in terms of eternal life and eternal death here and hereafter.

With the above thoughts in mind, we can see the truth of Schnackenburg's (1968:567) claim: 'Thus Johannine faith has a soteriological* as well as a Christological* character; the aspects are equally important and closely allied.'

CONCLUSION

As we prepare to reflect, in the solitude of retreat, on the spiritual journeys of some of the representative figures of the Fourth Gospel, let us pray each day for a stronger faith in Jesus so that 'through this belief [we] may have life in his name' (20:31).

THIRD PREPARATORY READING

IMAGINATION AND PRAYING THE GOSPELS

INTRODUCTORY REMARKS

Psychological research has drawn attention to the fact that human consciousness is experienced in two complementary modes — one associated with the left hemisphere of the brain which is predominantly logical, linear, sequential, analytic, objective and verbal and one associated with the right hemisphere of the brain which is predominantly intuitive, holistic, relational, synthetic, subjective and non-verbal.[1]

The highly-structured approach to education in most parts of the Western World has, in practice if not in theory, cultivated the former mode of consciousness at the considerable expense of the latter. Indeed, some educational institutions, even in these supposedly enlightened times, continue to be little more than echo factories in which the creative and imaginative capacities of the students are inhibited.

This generalisation is true also of some old but enduring forms of Christian religious education and catechesis

---

1 For a fuller and very readable treatment of the research findings, see Edwards (1981:19-43).

which tend to identify faith with intellectual assent to doctrinal statements and to equate prayer with the rather mechanical repetition of time-honoured formulas, often petitionary in character and lacking in immediacy.

For the right-brain mode of consciousness, on the other hand, a living faith is not so much a question of making room in one's head for more thoughts about God (important as that may be) as of making room in one's heart for God himself and for all who are created in God's image. The imaginative prayer which is congruent with such faith will have, as it were, a life of its own; it will be largely unstructured, attentive to God's presence, open to religious experience, and notably less verbal in character.

I believe that faith will always leave something to be desired if it does not involve the exercise of the imagination for the simple reason that authentic Christian faith is the activity of a person in his or her wholeness and necessarily engages not only the intellect but all the human faculties. Putting it more boldly, Gregory Baum (1975:244) states: 'While in classical theology it was supposed that faith resides in the intelligence, it may be more realistic ... to say that faith resides in the imagination.'

With good reason, therefore, does Fischer (1983:3) assert: 'The power of the imagination needs to be recovered above all in the daily life of Christians, in our reading of scripture, our attempts to pray, our efforts to make moral decisions.'

Within the brief compass of this book, we will have space to consider only the use of the imagination in prayer based on the Gospels. In the following section, two complementary approaches will be suggested which may be modified according to personal preference and the nature of the chosen text. For some readers this may entail the discovery of ways of praying that are new to them. For others, especially those familiar with the *Spiritual*

Exercises of St Ignatius of Loyola, it may involve rather the recovery or reaffirmation of old ones.

PRAYING THE GOSPELS IMAGINATIVELY

Taking account of the circumstances of our daily life, we should choose, on a regular basis, a time of day and a place which we find conducive to reflection on the word of God.[2] An allocation of 30 minutes is suggested; but this could be varied in the light of time constraints and other pertinent factors.

In selecting a text for contemplative prayer,[3] we could follow one of the 'reading plans' that are available in bookstores where Bibles are sold or we could work our way systematically through one of the Gospels. If we choose the Gospel prescribed for the liturgical cycle of the current year, we could correlate our private prayer with the public worship of the Church.

Identifying with a biblical character

Let us suppose that our scripture passage for the day is John 1:43-51 which records the call of two of Jesus' disciples, Philip and Nathanael. Our reflection might develop along these lines. For want of a better word, I will speak of steps; but I do not mean to imply thereby that

---

2 Practical details concerning the time and place for prayer are discussed in Cassidy (1980:60-85).
3 Most writers distinguish between the terms 'meditation' and 'contemplation' in ways which reflect the spiritual tradition (Carmelite, Jesuit, etc.) they espouse. For purposes of this essay, I will consider meditation to be a prayerful exercise which involves primarily the activity of the intellect and will and contemplation to be a prayerful exercise which has as its point of departure the human imagination. Though there are elements of both in the approaches to prayer outlined in these pages, the latter term is more generally descriptive of the method which is recommended.

we are engaged in something mechanical or inflexibly sequential.

Step 1: Begin with a few minutes of silence. Leave aside the cares of the moment; acknowledge the presence of God; and pray for the enlightenment of the Holy Spirit. We could make our own the words that Eli counselled the child Samuel to say, 'Speak, Lord, for your servant is listening' (1 Sam 3:9).

Step 2: Read the chosen passage slowly, preferably aloud, conscious of the feelings of the people who are involved and of the dramatic qualities of the situation. With a view to clearing our minds of distractions, it can be helpful to read the passage more than once.

Step 3: Replay the scene imaginatively in the present tense, adopting the stance of a participant rather than that of an observer. We should not be unduly concerned if we find this a little difficult or if our efforts lack the highly 'pictorial', even photographic, quality which seems to come easily to some people. Like liturgical music, which is intended to facilitate our entry into the sacred mysteries we celebrate, the exercise of our imagination in prayer is a means to our union with God and not an end in itself.

As he has a greater share of the action than Philip of Bethsaida, let us identify with Nathanael, the man from Cana in Galilee (cf. Jn 21:2).

In 'filling in' the details, we may find ourselves quite spontaneously addressing questions such as these: What is Nathanael doing under the fig tree to which Jesus will later make reference? Is he perhaps reading the Hebrew Scriptures as some commentators suggest? In addition to what is recorded in the text, what do Philip and Nathanael have to say to each another before they set about finding Jesus? Who else is present when Jesus speaks of Nathanael as a true Israelite? What is Nathanael's reaction to this quite unexpected encomium? What is his further reaction

Imagination and praying the Gospels

when Jesus claims to have seen him under the fig tree before Philip called? What does he make of Jesus' statement that he will, like Jacob (Israel) at Bethel (Gen 28:12), 'see the sky opened and the angels of God ascending and descending'?

Of course, we are not simply engaged in answering questions; this would suggest some intellectual pursuit. Our endeavour is rather to put ourselves into the midst of the action by standing in the shoes of the character of our choice and by entering as fully as our imagination will allow into his or her experience.

Step 4: Attend next to the personal agenda that presents itself as the reflection proceeds and as the word of the Lord speaks to us in the depths of our hearts. We may be challenged to admit our own religious prejudice as we identify with the initial scepticism of Nathanael. We may feel called to respond to Philip's invitation, 'Come and see', by resolving to set aside additional time for loving converse with our Lord, perhaps in the context of a spiritual retreat. We may be moved to make our own the titles that Nathanael employs in expressing his faith in Jesus, using them at the conclusion of our prayer as a kind of *mantra* (see below). We may, in the light of Philip's action in bringing Nathanael to Jesus, be prompted to reappraise the missionary quality of our own faith commitment.

If we keep a journal, some of the material that claims our attention at this time may be further 'processed' later when we come to write our entries for the day.[4]

Step 5: Conclude the period of contemplation with a brief prayer of thanksgiving and with an act of reverence for the sacred text (kissing the book perhaps as the priest does after proclaiming the Good News at Mass).

---

4 Useful information on journalling can be found in Simons (1978).

Depending upon the time available, a few minutes might be spent at the beginning of this concluding step in praying a mantra drawn from or based on the Gospel text. This simple exercise could be repeated later in the day as part of our evening prayer.

As a variant to the approach we have just outlined, but using basically the same five steps, we could picture ourselves among an audience of early Christians when their friend Nathanael responds to an invitation to share with them the story of his vocation. We listen attentively as he relates his personal myth* and tells of the event which radically changed the direction of his life and gave new meaning and purpose to it. If we wish, we may add our questions to those which are put to him by his fellow believers.

This variant has certain limitations; but it nonetheless calls our imagination into play and can, therefore, help us to move from the world of the protagonist to the inner world of our own psyche.

Identifying with Jesus

Just as we can identify with Nathanael or with one of the other people who encounter Jesus, so also can we identify with Jesus himself. This will help us in our quest to 'make [our] own the mind of Christ Jesus' (Phil 2:5 NJB).

We could use this approach occasionally as an alternative to the one presented above; or, if we can find time for a second period of imaginative prayer (which should be easy during a retreat), we could use it later in the day as a follow-up to our initial reflection on the Gospel narrative.

The same methodology may be followed as before. However, in this case, I recommend that we identify with Jesus not at the historical moment of the events recorded

Imagination and praying the Gospels

by John but at the time he retires from the scene to some solitary place in the late evening to reflect upon these and other events of his day in the company of his Father.[5]

This is rather like being present when Jesus makes what we would call, in today's terminology, his examination* of consciousness.[6]

What are his thoughts about his first encounter with Nathanael who hails from a village not far from his own and who, after a shaky beginning, has become his disciple? What are his impressions of this man whom Philip has brought to him? In what terms does he commend him and his other new disciples to his Father? What plans does he have for this 'true Israelite' in whom there is 'no duplicity'?

It is not fanciful to suggest that Jesus prayed for the people whom he encountered on his earthly journey. Indeed, the Gospels furnish us with a number of examples (Lk 22:31-32 — Peter; Lk 23:34 — his executioners), the most notable of which is to be found in the 17th chapter of St John's Gospel in what has been called from the 16th century 'the high priestly prayer'. There Jesus prays at length for his disciples and 'also for those who will believe in [him] through their word' (Jn 17:20). These are the terms in which he continues in glory to make intercession for us (Rom 8:34; Heb 7:25; cf. Rom 8:26-27).

As we share with Jesus these sacred moments when he opens his heart to the one who sent him and whose holy will he does in all things (cf. Jn 5:30), we may present to him with confidence the concerns that now arise or that

---

5 Though we speak of the 'historical moment' of the events which are the subject of our reflection, we need to take account of the tremendous fact that, in contemplative prayer (as in liturgical celebration), we enter into sacred mysteries which are eternally present to the risen Christ. We encounter the *then* of history in the *now* of faith.
6 Refer to the seminal article by Aschenbrenner (1972).

came to the surface as we reflected on the experience of Nathanael.

This approach to the biblical text is useful with respect to many of the narrative passages of the four Gospels; but it can also be adapted fairly easily to the discourses of Jesus.

IMAGINATION OR MAKE-BELIEVE?

The objection is sometimes raised that the exercise of our imaginative faculty in prayer could easily lead us away from the 'real' world into an irrational world of fruitless, even dangerous, make-believe or escapist fantasy.

There would be something to be said for this position if the focus of our imagination were the imaginary which, by definition, has no basis in fact. However, we are engaged in what Amos Wilder would call 'imagining the real'.[7] This is the kind of activity which, in the scientific world, has given rise to great discoveries and inventions.

More worthy of serious attention than those who equate the imaginative with the irrational is Gula (1984:301) who writes:

> The imagination does not separate us from the facts, but helps illumine the facts so that we can see more than meets the eye. The imagination sees with the heart. For this reason, the most effective approach to the biblical story for spiritual growth is not an intellectual grasp of concepts about God or Jesus but the imaginative play between the text and our experience through which we come to know God and Jesus with our hearts.

Such aberrations as are possible derive not from the nature of imaginative prayer itself but from certain predispositions on the part of the one praying. For this

---

[7] This is the title of a book by Wilder published by Possum Press in 1978.

Imagination and praying the Gospels 73

reason, as with so many aspects of the spiritual life, the assistance of a prudent 'soul-friend' or of a competent director,[8] skilled in the art of discernment, has much to recommend it.

A good guide is provided by Sheldrake (1987:109) who says, with reference to the images that emerge from Gospel contemplation, that 'what produces joy, harmony and growth is the gift of the good spirit, and that which produces sadness, despair or fragmentation is (to use Ignatius's language) a temptation of the evil spirit.'

THE FRUITS OF IMAGINATIVE PRAYER

Some of the fruits of imaginative prayer based on the Gospels are implicit in what has been written so far. However, it will be helpful if we spell them out in a little more detail so that the potential of regular reflective prayer of this kind may be more fully appreciated.

Firstly, to enter prayerfully, attentively and imaginatively into the past world of the Jesus of history is to open ourselves to the discovery of new possibilities in our relationship with the Christ of faith in the present. This can be both a very challenging and a very enlightening experience.

Secondly, and more specifically, imaginative scriptural prayer, far from diverting us into a world of illusion and unreality, can provide us with access to important and hitherto insufficiently explored dimensions of reality which are not susceptible of empirical verification, including the deeper levels of our own uniquely personal being. We may learn experientially that 'the word of God is living and effective, sharper than any two-edged sword, penetrating

---

8 Useful follow-up reading on the topic of spiritual direction can be found in Edwards (1980), Leech (1980), and Seller (1990).

even between soul and spirit, joints and marrow, and able to discern reflections and thoughts of the heart' (Heb 4:12).

The meaning that we are ultimately exposed to is not just the meaning of this or that text of Sacred Scripture (important as that may be) but the meaning of our own very selves. 'In reality', as we read in the conciliar document, *Gaudium et spes** (22), 'it is only in the mystery of the Word made flesh that the mystery of [the human person] truly becomes clear' (Flannery 1975:922).

Thirdly, inasmuch as the events in the life of Jesus and in the lives of those who experienced his saving ministry find their resonance in 'the joy and hope, the grief and anguish' (cf. GS, 1) of Christians today, imaginative reflection on them can be not only self-revelatory but liberating. In Sheldrake's (1987:107) very pertinent words:

> It can free a person to allow deep-rooted feelings to emerge which are blocking any further growth. Imaginative contemplation, when it progresses naturally, takes on a life of its own — and the life is that of the person praying.

Fourthly, as we come to realise that the Gospel story and our own story are mutually illuminating, our horizons will be extended. Against this wider backdrop, we will be challenged to ongoing conversion in our own lives and to greater social consciousness in all that regards the lives of our neighbours. Having stood in the shoes of some of the biblical characters, we will find it easier to stand in the shoes of our contemporaries.

Fifthly, if we have any responsibility, as a parent or as a teacher, for ministering to young people in their spiritual quest, we have in Gospel contemplation a method of prayer to which many of them, in my experience, respond with enthusiasm.

CONCLUDING REMARKS

The best piece of advice on prayer that I have come across is the much-quoted reply of the esteemed spiritual director, Abbot John Chapman, to a nun who had sought his assistance: 'Pray as you can and not as you can't.' With this in mind, I would be slow to suggest that what has been proposed in these pages will meet with the unqualified approval of all readers without exception. As was indicated in the Introduction, different personality types are more at home with one form of prayer than with another.

I will leave the last word to another master of the spiritual life, St John Climacus: 'Authentic prayer', he writes, 'can never be learnt from someone else. It has its own instructor within it. Prayer is God's gift to the one who prays.'

DAY ONE

JESUS AND NICODEMUS
(John 3:1-21,31-36; 7:37-52; 19:38-42)

1. REFLECTIVE STUDY OF THE TEXT

Introduction

Let us begin our day in the company of Jesus, Nicodemus and John the Evangelist with a few moments of silent prayer, recalling the presence of God and asking for the enlightenment of the Holy Spirit. You may like to conclude your prayer as follows:

> Lord, may everything I do today begin with your inspiration, continue with your help, and reach a fruitful conclusion under the guidance of your Holy Spirit. Amen.

Read all three texts cited above aloud and slowly, keeping in mind that we have in them the word of God in the words of John. As Sheldrake (1987:115) says:

> The gospel texts are the result of a particular writer's experience of the risen Christ, related to the various traditions which the writer has inherited about the Jesus of history.... Our access to Jesus through scripture prayer or reading is always mediated through the perspective of the gospel writer ....

Read them aloud a second time as they appear in the detailed commentary below; and do not be slow to enter into dialogue with the writer. With good reason, one might ask him: What kind of a man for you was Nicodemus? Why did you include his story in your Gospel? What particular needs of your community did you have in mind?

Before proceeding with your first prayerfully studious encounter with the text, a few preliminary observations of a more general nature might be helpful.

Preliminary observations

The hand of John is very much in evidence in the narrative of Jesus' meeting with Nicodemus; for the style, the vocabulary and the theology are distinctively Johannine. Collins (1977:1413) observes: '... [W]e are dealing with a passage which has every likelihood of providing a compendium of Johannine thought, of being, in effect, a brief synopsis of the Gospel itself.'

If we accept that Nicodemus finally became a disciple of Jesus (and not all commentators do), we have in his successive appearances in the Gospel at least the first steps in a spiritual journey from curiosity to commitment. Read this way, his story is the record of a conversion, of a 'blessed defeat' to use C.S. Lewis's words.

Who is Rabbi Nicodemus?

Mentioned only in the Fourth Gospel, he is not a major character if we judge by the number of verses in which he is centre-stage; but he is by no means an unimportant one. Indeed, the author has tied together the three appearances of Nicodemus in such a way that his character, if not fully rounded, is nonetheless subtly delineated.

Day One

We know from the text that he is a Pharisee[1] (3:1; 7:50), a teacher (3:10), and one of the seventy members of the supreme religious court called the Sanhedrin* (3:1). He is, therefore, a powerful and influential member of the Jewish establishment. In keeping with his high office, he is attentive to the Law* (7:50-51) and mindful of the demands of ritual piety (19:39-40).

A representative figure

Like so many other characters in John's account of the Good News, Nicodemus is a representative figure. Initially (that is, in 3:1-21), it would seem that he typifies those people of some standing in society whose attraction to Jesus falls short of a true commitment in faith. This is highlighted by the fact that his first appearance is sandwiched between the stories of the guileless Nathanael who confesses Jesus with several titles (1:49) and the 'heretic' Samaritan woman who also comes to faith (4:29,42). At this point he is close to the 'kingdom of God'* of which Jesus speaks; but he cannot bring himself to confess.

Schneiders (1987a:191), who is careful to distinguish the role of Nicodemus in the Johannine church from his role in the Gospel, writes with considerable insight:

> No doubt Nicodemus functioned in *John's community* as the hero of the Jewish Christian members, but his primary function in the *Gospel* is to catch the conscience of the reader. Nicodemus is the very type of the truly religious person who is, on the one hand, utterly sincere and, on the other, complacent about his or her knowledge of God and God's will. Such people are basically closed to God's revelation.

---

1   It is possible that the reference to Nicodemus's membership of the Sanhedrin may be anachronistic because, in Jesus' day, that elite body was closely connected with the Temple priesthood. It was only after the destruction of the Temple in 70 C.E. that Pharisees came into their own as the dominant force in Jewish society.

Nicodemus and the rich young ruler

Some commentators have suggested that the narrative of Nicodemus's encounter with Jesus may have been derived, at least in part, from the Synoptic* tradition where its analogue is the account of the rich young man (Mt 19:16-30 // Mk 10:17-31 // Lk 18:18-30). It also has some affinities with the discussion between Jesus and the lawyer concerning the greatest commandment, particularly in the Lucan version (Mt 22:34-40 // Mk 12:28-31 // Lk 10:25-28).

Both Nicodemus and the rich young man take the initiative in approaching Jesus; both address him as 'teacher'; and both lack the faith to respond positively to his challenge. More significantly, the conversation focuses on 'eternal life' (cf. Mt 19:16 // Mk 10:17 // Lk 18:18).

In view of the fact that 'Nicodemus' is a word of Greek origin signifying 'ruler' or 'conqueror', it is interesting to note that Luke identifies the young man as a 'ruler' (Lk 18:18).

Let us now turn our attention to the commentary. As your time is limited, there is no need to look up all the references that have been provided. That could be left to follow-up study at a later date. For the present, avoid any 'busyness' which would detract from the climate of recollection you seek to maintain.

If you find the session too long, please feel free to stop and catch your breath at a convenient place.

Detailed commentary

(a) The mystery of rebirth[2] (3:1-8)

[1]Now there was a Pharisee named Nicodemus, a ruler of the Jews. [2]He came to Jesus at night and said to him,

---

2 The headings that have been employed in dividing the material on Nicodemus have been taken from Bultmann's classic commentary on John (see bibliography).

Day One

'Rabbi, we know that you are a teacher who has come from God, for no one can do these signs that you are doing unless God is with him.' ³Jesus answered and said to him, 'Amen, amen, I say to you, no one can see the kingdom of God without being born from above.' ⁴Nicodemus said to him, 'How can a person once grown old be born again? Surely he cannot re-enter his mother's womb and be born again, can he?' ⁵Jesus answered, 'Amen, amen, I say to you, no one can enter the kingdom of God without being born of water and Spirit. ⁶What is born of flesh is flesh and what is born of spirit is spirit. ⁷Do not be amazed that I told you, "You must be born from above." ⁸The wind blows where it wills, and you can hear the sound it makes, but you do not know where it comes from or where it goes; so it is with everyone who is born of the Spirit.'

The concluding verses of the previous chapter (2:23-25), with their reference to the inadequacy of faith based on signs or miracles, set the scene for the dialogue between Jesus and the teacher of Israel and, at the same time, preserve the narrative continuity of the Gospel text.

Unlike the meeting between Jesus and the woman of Samaria, the meeting between Jesus and Nicodemus is not a chance encounter. Nicodemus, whom John is at pains to identify with official Judaism from the outset, acts on his own initiative in seeking Jesus out. He comes under cover of darkness to escape detection by the Jewish establishment, no doubt sharing the fears of people like Joseph of Arimathea (19:38). Later, when we meet Nicodemus again at the burial of Jesus, he will be identified as 'the one who had first come to him at night' (19:39).

We have no way of knowing for certain whether he has come alone or, as was often the case among the rabbis, accompanied by his students. Whatever the situation, John is alive to the dramatic potential of a one-to-one confrontation.

The phrase 'at night' may have a merely temporal reference because the rabbis commonly discussed the Torah* well into the evening which, as the Talmud* says, was made for study. However, given the fact that light and darkness are characteristic themes of the Fourth Gospel (cf. 3:19-21), the writer's intention may be symbolic (cf. 13:30 — the departure of Judas) — an interpretation which is supported by Nicodemus's lack of understanding of what Jesus has to say.

With this in mind, we might almost apply to him what Jesus says in another context (the raising of Lazarus): 'But if one walks at night, he stumbles, because the light is not in him' (11:10).

Like Nathanael (1:49) and the disciples of John the Baptist (1:38), he accords Jesus the courtesy title of rabbi; but unlike them he does not proceed to give Jesus any title indicative of growing faith in him.

With unconscious irony, which he will appreciate only with the wisdom of hindsight, Nicodemus begins by saying, 'We know that you are a teacher who has come from God' (3:2; cf. 9:33) — a conclusion he has arrived at, on his own admission, on the basis of Jesus' signs. 'For no one', he adds, 'can do these signs that you are doing unless God is with him.'

However, as was suggested above with reference to 2:23-25, 'signs faith' is far from adequate; and, for this reason, Collins (1977:1411) can write with some justification: 'It appears more likely that the evangelist has selected Nicodemus as a representative figure to describe a type of belief that is insufficient for salvation.'

In any case, we need hardly be reminded of the fact that many who see Jesus' signs (Judas among them) eventually reject him (cf. 6:60-66).

We might ask who the 'we' are for whom Nicodemus claims to speak. He may be presumptuous enough to

Day One 83

speak on behalf of the Sanhedrin or of the Jewish people as a whole; but it is possible that he speaks for disciples who have accompanied him and whose presence the writer ignores for dramatic reasons.

Later in the discussion Jesus turns these words, 'we know you are a teacher', back on Nicodemus. 'You are the teacher of Israel', Jesus says, 'and you do not understand this?' (3:10). It is a gentle reproof, reinforced by Jesus' confident assertion, 'We [on the other hand] speak of what we know.' Do we have here shades of the early Christian-Jewish polemic at the time of the Johannine community, a thinly veiled dialogue betweeen the church and the synagogue?

Presupposed in Jesus' rather enigmatic response to Nicodemus's introductory remarks is the question, actually unasked by his interlocutor but of concern to many of the Jews: 'What must I do to inherit eternal life?' (Lk 18:18 // Mt 19:16 // Mk 10:17). 'No one can see the kingdom of God', says Jesus, 'without being born from above.'[3]

Jesus' absolute statement about the need to be born from above if one is to see (or 'enter', as in 3:5) the kingdom of God is not unlike the other radical claims he makes about what is required if one would attain 'eternal life' (in John's preferred terminology). To take but the most obvious example: 'Amen, amen, I say to you, unless you eat the flesh of the Son of Man and drink his blood, you do not have life within you. Whoever eats my flesh and drinks my blood has eternal life and I will raise him up on the last day' (6:53-54; cf. 7:24; 13:8).

---

[3] Note in passing that we find in this narrative the only two references in the Fourth Gospel to the 'kingdom [or, more dynamically, "reign"] of God' (3:3,5). Where the Synoptic writers (especially Matthew) speak of the kingdom, John presents the King. This is very much in evidence in his account of the passion and death of Jesus.

The theme of the kingdom or reign of God would have been known to John, as well as to Jesus himself and to Nicodemus, from the apocalyptic* literature of late Judaism. It epitomised Israel's hope in a future event which would constitute the Lord's definitive intervention in human history — a hope which had become increasingly politicised (cf. Lk:24). Understandably, in the preaching of the early Church, this supreme manifestation of the Lord's kingly power was related directly to the saving mission of Jesus.

Nicodemus, in keeping with rabbinic pedagogical practice, raises an objection to Jesus' words. 'How can a person once grown old be born again?' he asks. 'Surely he cannot re-enter his mother's womb and be born again, can he?' He clearly misunderstands what Jesus has said.

Some commentators see the source of this misunderstanding in the fact that the Greek word *anōthen* can mean both 'again' and 'from above'. In this interpretation, as the revised New American Bible translation brings out, Jesus is speaking about spiritual rebirth from above; but Nicodemus takes rebirth in the literal, physical sense.

Questioning this approach, Schneiders (1987a:192) observes: 'Johannine misunderstanding is based on misplaced literalness in interpreting what is said, not on a failure to understand the actual words.' She suggests as a possible reading for *anōthen* the word 'anew' which does not necessarily imply a second time.

Another point of view (one which, in the light of 3:10, cannot be cogently defended) is that Nicodemus is speaking rhetorically about the possibility of beginning life over again — that is, with a clean slate morally speaking.

Culpepper's (1983:135) comment on these verses is one which would be acceptable, I believe, to most exegetes*: 'As with all of the Johannine misunderstandings, Nicodemus here serves as a foil which enables Jesus to explain his meaning while vaulting the reader to an elevated position of superiority over the character's limited understanding.'

In passing, we may remark that rebirth is a common theme in Christian writing (see, for example, 1 Pet 1:3,22-23; Jas 1:18; 1 Cor 3:1-2; 2 Cor 5:17; Gal 6:15; Heb 5:12-14). It is an image specially dear to self-styled 'born again' Christians for whom it identifies the privileged moment of their conversion to Christ.

There is more to it than that, however; and it is on the words 'of water and Spirit' (3:5), which Jesus adds to his original challenge to Nicodemus (3:3), that we should focus our attention if we would understand the fuller meaning of Christian rebirth.

No doubt, for members of John's community, these words would have had baptismal overtones (cf. 1:32-33); but, as O'Day (1988:57) rightly argues, they must first be comprehensible, free of sacramental allusiveness, in the narrative context in which they are uttered by Jesus and heard by Nicodemus.

The interpretation which most commends itself to me is one which understands water as having reference to the issue of maternal fluid which accompanies childbirth. This would help to clarify the contrast which Jesus makes in his rather cryptic statement in the following verse (3:6), 'What is born of flesh is flesh and what is born of spirit is spirit.' In the words of Sandra Schneiders (1987a:192): 'There are two births, one of water and another of spirit. The first is human birth of flesh from flesh; the second is spiritual birth of spirit from spirit.'

Ultimately, Nicodemus is being called upon to redefine the Covenant*, to acknowledge that it is not sufficient merely to be of the number of Abraham's children (cf. 8:31-41). With a new heart and a new spirit (cf. Ezek 36:25-27), he must embrace not only the Law which was given through Moses but also the grace and truth which come through Jesus (1:17). To quote Schneiders (1987a:193) again: 'He is being challenged to recognise the arrival of the New Covenant in the person of Jesus whose signs are meant to draw him into relationship with this Teacher-Revealer who surpasses Moses.'

Sensing Nicodemus's resistance or perhaps his need for reassurance (cf. 5:28; 1 Jn 3:13), Jesus continues, 'Do not be amazed that I told you, "You must be born from above."' The 'you' is plural in the Greek text — a nice touch; for Jesus' words, as the evangelist knows, have a universal application.

Then, incorporating what was probably a well-known proverb in his day, Jesus adds: 'The wind blows where it wills, and you can hear the sound it makes, but you do not know where it comes from or where it goes; so it is with everyone who is born of the Spirit.' He thus underlines the absolute gratuity of God's gift of rebirth to eternal life.

Like the wind, the Spirit is recognisable through its effects; and Spirit-filled people are known through their deeds (cf. 1 Jn 3:9-10; 4:7,12-13; 5:18).

(b) The mystery of the Son of Man (3:9-21)
Part 1: (3:9-15)

[9]Nicodemus answered and said to him, 'How can this happen?' [10]Jesus answered and said to him, 'You are the teacher of Israel and you do not understand this? [11]Amen, amen, I say to you, we speak of what we know and we testify to what we have seen, but you people do not accept our testimony. [12]If I tell you about earthly things and you do not believe, how will you believe if I tell you about heavenly things? [13]No one has gone up to heaven except the one who has come down from heaven, the Son of Man. [14]And just as Moses lifted up

the serpent in the desert, so must the Son of Man be lifted up, [15]so that everyone who believes in him may have eternal life.'

Compared with the Samaritan woman and the man born blind, Nicodemus does not have a great deal to say. He asks a further question, 'How can this happen?' (cf. Gen 18:12; Lk 1:37), which is both a restatement of his earlier protest (3:4) and Jesus' cue to extend his discourse, and then effectively disappears from the scene. In response to Jesus' question in 3:10 he is silent. Dialogue has become monologue.

Jesus gently chides him as a rabbi might rebuke a presumptuous or arrogant student. Nicodemus is 'the teacher of Israel' who does not know earthly things let alone those of heaven.

'We testify to what we have seen,' says Jesus, 'but you people do not accept our testimony.' The words have an apologetic* ring to them and are reminiscent of the introduction to the first of the Johannine epistles:

> What was from the beginning,
> what we have heard,
> what we have seen with our eyes,
> ... what we have seen and heard
> we proclaim now to you (1 Jn 1:1,3).

It could be, according to Ellis (1984:55), that 'in 3:11-12, John has Jesus speak through Nicodemus to his Jewish readers on the fence at the end of the first century.' The 'we' includes both Jesus and the disciples who will later teach in his name.

They witness to the truth, but their message falls on deaf ears as far as 'the Jews' are concerned (cf. 1:11; 3:32; 5:43; 12:37). Herein lies the basic and most disturbing irony of the Fourth Gospel, that those who have waited so long for the advent of the Messiah do not recognise him when he comes in the person of Jesus of Nazareth.

Jesus passes judgment on Nicodemus but he does not close the door. Nicodemus's *kairos** moment will come only after the Son of Man has been lifted up when he goes down into the tomb with him (19:39-42).

Here, as elsewhere in John's Gospel (1:47; 2:24; 5:6; 6:6,15,61,64,70-71; 13:1,11; 16:19,30; 18:4; 19:28), Jesus lays claim to superior knowledge. He presents himself as one who speaks with authority not only about 'earthly things' but also about 'heavenly things'. 'No one', he states by way of justification, 'has gone up to heaven except the one who has come down from heaven, the Son of Man' (3:13; cf. Prov 30:4). He is, in a fuller sense than Nicodemus can possibly know, 'a teacher who has come from God' (3:2).

John's community, because they have been born of the Spirit, have access to this heavenly knowledge. They have seen the 'greater things' of which Jesus spoke to Nathanael (cf. 1:50-51). They know and bear witness to the fact that Jesus Christ is the unique Son of God, the pre-existent Son of Man (1:1-2; 6:62).

To explicate the saving role of this heavenly Son of Man, Jesus makes use of an image drawn from the history of his people. The bronze serpent which Moses raised on a pole (Num 21:4-9; cf. Wis 16:5-7) was a source of salvation to those who had been bitten by serpents in the wilderness. Lifted up on the cross, Jesus will be the saviour of all who will look to him with the eyes of faith, to 'everyone who believes in him' (3:15).[4]

Keep in mind that the phrase 'lifted up' (see, too, 8:28; 12:32,34) is John's way of describing both the crucifixion

---

4 Apropos of this teaching, Schnackenburg (1968:396) comments: 'The point of the comparison is neither the stake nor the serpent but the "exaltation". And this is linked with the thought that salvation for many comes from this "exaltation".'

of Jesus and his exaltation (cf. Acts 2:33-36; 5:30-31; Phil 2:8-11) to God's right hand. Lifted up in shame, he is uplifted in glory. We might see this as the Johannine equivalent and theological development of the passion and resurrection predictions in the Synoptic Gospels (Mt 16:21 // Mk 8:31 // Lk 9:22).

In saying that faith in a crucified redeemer is needed if one is to enjoy eternal life (that is, 'enter the kingdom of God' — 3:3,5), Jesus finally answers Nicodemus's question, 'How can this happen?' (3:9).

The expression, 'eternal life' (qualitative), which is used here for the first of 17 times in this Gospel, means more than just 'everlasting life' (quantitative). It is a sharing in the very life of God both here and hereafter.

Part 2 (3:16-21)

[16] For God so loved the world that he gave his only Son, so that everyone who believes in him might not perish but might have eternal life. [17] For God did not send his Son into the world to condemn the world, but that the world might be saved through him. [18] Whoever believes in him will not be condemned, but whoever does not believe has already been condemned, because he has not believed in the name of the only Son of God. [19] And this is the verdict, that the light came into the world, but people preferred darkness to light because their works were evil. [20] For everyone who does wicked things hates the light and does not come toward the light, so that his works might not be exposed. [21] But whoever lives the truth comes to the light, so that his works may be clearly seen as done in God.

In the revised edition of the New American Bible the above passage, 3:16-21, has no longer been enclosed in quotation marks. A case can be made for this seemingly minor revision on the grounds that these words may be presented just as acceptably as the evangelist's commentary on the teaching of Jesus as the very words of Jesus himself.

It begins with a statement which gives us the Good News in a nutshell. As McPolin (1979:35) expresses it:

> Thus the breadth of God's love is the world of mankind for whom Christ died and the depth of his love is his most precious gift, his only beloved Son, whose whole life, especially his death, reveals how much God wants to share his own 'eternal life' with mankind.

Behind every initiative of Jesus there is the prior initiative of a loving Father. It is this love which Jesus makes manifest in all that he says and does.

If the Church is catholic, it is not because it exists worldwide but because the mission it has received from Jesus bespeaks love for all humankind.

'God so loved the world that he *gave* his only Son.' The choice of the verb 'gave' is interesting because the writer usually, and very frequently, speaks of the Father's 'sending' Jesus (cf. 3:17). Read together with the words 'only Son', it is suggestive of God's call to Abraham to sacrifice Isaac: 'Take your son Isaac, your only one, whom you love, and go to the land of Moriah. There you shall offer him up as a holocaust on a height that I will point out to you' (Gen 22:2). In this connection, it is pertinent to note that only in John's Gospel does Jesus himself carry the wood of the cross up the hill of Calvary (19:17; cf. Mt 27:32 // Mk 15:21 // Lk 23:26).

A brief comment on the word 'world' might also be in order. It sometimes has a negative connotation in John as a symbol for those who are perverse in their unbelief; but it is obviously used positively in this context.

The theme of judgment, a notable one in the Fourth Gospel (see especially 5:22-30), is now introduced; and the commentary becomes more strongly polemical in character (cf. 12:47-48). Unlike the Samaritans who profess their belief in Jesus as 'the savior of the world' (4:42), 'the Jews' do not believe 'in the name of the only Son of God' (3:18).

Nicodemus's continued presence may be implied in what is said in this section of the text; but it is more likely that these words of judgment reflect the struggle that John's community was having with 'the Jews' and with defectors from its own ranks.

'Judgment', as Schnackenburg (1968:401) so well expresses it, 'is only the dark, reverse side of God's eschatological* act of love and redemption.' The love is God's initiative: the unbelief which invites judgment is ours. Condemnation is not God's purpose but our choice in preferring darkness to light.

These verses should serve to remind us that, while there are a number of judgment scenes in John, it is Jesus who ultimately passes judgment on his adversaries rather than vice versa.[5] 'Nor does the Father judge anyone, but he has given all judgment to his Son' (5:22).

If there is one thing that the evangelist stresses time and time again, it is that a response in faith is critical. To enjoy eternal life we must 'come toward the light', as he puts it here, and 'accomplish the works of God' (6:28) by believing in the one he has sent (6:29). If we are followers of Jesus, who is 'the light of the world' (8:12; 9:5), we 'will not walk in darkness, but will have the light of life' (8:12).

In a word, we will live the truth (cf. 3:21; 1 Jn 1:6).

---

[5] Neyrey (1981:117) supports this view: 'Subsequent dialogues are true judgment scenes in another sense [than the implied judgment of the ruler Nicodemus on Jesus]: the Jews confront the Johannine church and put it on trial. In each of these confrontations a curious pattern emerges in that the judged one becomes the Judge and those judging are judged.'

(c) The mystery of the witness (3:31-36)

³¹The one who comes from above is above all. The one who is of the earth is earthly and speaks of earthly things. But the one who comes from heaven [is above all]. ³²He testifies to what he has seen and heard, but no one accepts his testimony. ³³Whoever does accept his testimony certifies that God is trustworthy. ³⁴For the one whom God sent speaks the words of God. He does not ration his gift of the Spirit. ³⁵The Father loves the Son and has given everything over to him. ³⁶Whoever believes in the Son has eternal life, but whoever disobeys the Son will not see life, but the wrath of God remains upon him.

Before these verses, the writer includes the final witness of John the Baptist (3:22-30). It may appear to be rather out of place here; but a case could be made for the suggestion that the Baptist has been reintroduced to clarify the meaning of 'being born again of water and Spirit' (3:5), one of the key sacramental references in the Gospel.

It is interesting to note that, in the revised edition (1986) of the New Testament of the New American Bible, the above passage (3:31-36) has no longer been placed between quotation marks under the heading 'Discourse Concluded'. This fact (together with an explanatory footnote) indicates that the editor cannot be sure that it records the *ipsissima verba** of Jesus. It is most likely a continuation of the evangelist's reflection on the Lord's teaching (see 3:16-21).

As it summarises the main theological themes of the chapter, a detailed commentary hardly seems called for. Like a number of other passages in the Fourth Gospel (for example, 11:51-52; 12:16,33; 18:32; 20:30-31), it is addressed directly to the reader.

The final verse, which takes up the profound message of 3:15-16, is itself a beautiful summary of the entire chapter: 'Whoever believes in the Son has eternal life, but

Day One 93

whoever disobeys the Son will not see life, but the wrath of God remains upon him.' (Note the use of the present tense).

(d) Nicodemus's defence of Jesus (7:50-52)

> [50]Nicodemus, one of their members who had come to him earlier, said to them, [51]'Does our law condemn a person before it first hears him and finds out what he is doing?' [52]They answered and said to him, 'You are not from Galilee also, are you? Look and see that no prophet arises from Galilee.'

At the Feast of Tabernacles*, many people in the crowd begin to believe in Jesus. Impressed, as Nicodemus claims to have been by Jesus' signs (3:2), they say, 'When the Messiah comes, will he perform more signs than this man has done?' (7:31). There is a division among them, however, concerning the Davidic lineage of the Messiah (7:40-44).

The response of the Pharisees and the chief priests to this unwelcome enthusiasm is to send guards to arrest Jesus (7:32). Their mission is a failure; indeed, the guards return sharing the sentiments of those who had been moved by his teaching: 'Never before has anyone spoken like this one' (7:46).

At this point Nicodemus re-enters the story. He reappears, in fact, soon after Jesus has spoken to the people about the 'living water' (7:38) — that is, the Spirit (7:39) — which is his gift to those who believe in him. In this way, the writer skilfully links his material with the earlier passage in which Jesus speaks to Nicodemus about the need to be 'born of water and Spirit' (3:5).

His final appearance, at the kingly burial of Jesus, will take place immediately following the climactic scene in which Jesus dies 'lifted up' (cf. 3:4) on the cross. Then it is that Jesus hands over the spirit (19:30) and blood and water flow from his pierced side (19:34).

It must be difficult for Nicodemus to speak up in defence of Jesus in the presence of his peers, the more so in view of their vituperative questioning of the guards whom they ask, 'Have you also been deceived? Have any of the authorities or the Pharisees believed in him?' This time perhaps the irony is not lost of the 'teacher of Israel'.

If he does believe in Jesus, he does not say so. Nor is there any record of his intervening on another occasion when (presuming that Nicodemus is present) Caiaphas says to the Sanhedrin: 'You know nothing, nor do you consider that it is better that one man should die instead of the people, so that the whole nation may not perish' (11:49-50).

(e) The burial of Jesus (19:38-42)

> [38]After this, Joseph of Arimathea, secretly a disciple of Jesus for fear of the Jews, asked Pilate if he could remove the body of Jesus. And Pilate permitted it. So he came and took his body. [39]Nicodemus, the one who had first come to him at night, also came bringing a mixture of myrrh and aloes weighing about one hundred pounds. [40]They took the body of Jesus and bound it with burial cloths along with the spices, according to the Jewish burial custom. [41]Now in the place where he had been crucified, there was a garden, and in the garden a new tomb, in which no one had yet been buried. [42]So they laid Jesus there because of the Jewish preparation day; for the tomb was close by.

This final appearance of Nicodemus is also linked with chapter 3 by the reminder that he is 'the one who had first come to [Jesus] at night' (see 3:2 and 7:50).

In John's version of the burial of Jesus, it is Nicodemus the Pharisee who brings the material with which to anoint the body of Jesus (cf. Mk 16:1; Lk 24:1). What is especially noteworthy is the huge quantity of myrrh and aloes that he brings for this hurried burial — 'about 100 pounds'. This detail is consistent with John's portrayal of Jesus as a king (for only a king would be buried in this fashion); but the truth of the statement is surely theological rather than historical.

What is the status of Nicodemus at this time? Has he come to understand at last (cf. 3:10)? Joseph of Arimathea is said to be 'a disciple of Jesus', though a secret one for fear of 'the Jews'; but the same is not explicitly stated of Nicodemus. Is it reasonable, however, to suppose that he has finally 'come to the light' (3:20) and has been drawn in faith to the one who said, 'And when I am lifted up from the earth, I will draw everyone to myself' (12:32)?

In any event, he remains for us, who identify with him as we read his story, 'the symbol of every believer, coming with questions to the Lord, opening himself to possibilities of new truth about the Lord and therefore about himself' (Suggit 1981:105).

We have Jesus' assurance that no one who comes to him will ever be rejected (6:37).

2. IMAGINATIVE PRAYER WITH NICODEMUS

The following suggestions for entering imaginatively into the experience of Nicodemus are not meant to be adopted uncritically. They are only guidelines to be read quickly and then set aside as you stand in the shoes of the Pharisee and bring your own imagination to bear on the three important episodes of his faith journey recorded by John.

Though I speak about Nicodemus in the third person, it will be much more effective if, during this time of prayer, you identify with him as fully as possible by using his words and thinking his thoughts (first person, present tense). Never lose sight of the fact that the use of the imagination in this way is not an end in itself but a means to dialogue with Jesus now present to us in faith.

Nicodemus at home. Picture Nicodemus in his home reflecting on what he has heard from so many sources about the teaching of Jesus and about the signs that this man from Nazareth is purported to have worked. Perhaps he is even now discussing the impact of this wonder-worker with Joseph of Arimathea or one of his other colleagues from the Sanhedrin.

His curiosity aroused, Nicodemus debates with himself the pros and cons of meeting this increasingly controversial figure. He is conscious of the fact that a man of his status and wealth could stand to lose much by such an encounter. It would hardly be looked on with favour by those whom he has heard speaking dismissively of Jesus.

The night meeting. Make your way to Jesus' dwelling with Nicodemus under cover of darkness. What are his feelings as he crosses the town from his own more well-to-do area? What questions is he turning over in his mind that he plans to put to Jesus?

Imaginatively recreate the meeting with Jesus. How does Jesus greet him (warmly, with surprise, perhaps cautiously, ...)? How does he react to Jesus' rather cryptic statement about the need to be born again? What is his estimate of Jesus personally? In what frame of mind does he leave for home? Make the return journey with him. What thoughts exercise his mind as he retires for the night? Has curiosity given way to credence? Has the visit created more 'problems' than it solved?

The meeting of the authorities. You are present when the guards sent to arrest Jesus are confronted by the authorities. Listen while they are interrogated with scant respect by the chief priests and Pharisees. What are Nicodemus's feelings during this interchange? What is his reaction to the guards' observation concerning Jesus, 'Never before has anyone spoken like this one'?

Day One

Nicodemus pleads that Jesus be given a fair hearing by those who do not share the enthusiasm or the judgment of the guards. How difficult is it for him to make this intervention? What are his feelings as the scorn of his colleagues is now directed towards him? Does he pursue the matter later with one of them, Joseph of Arimathea perhaps? Does he, before this day is out, revise his ideas about the cost of discipleship?

The burial of Jesus. Joseph of Arimathea approaches Pilate to request permission to remove the body of Jesus, preparatory to burial. He acquaints his friend Nicodemus of his plans.

What is stirring in the mind and heart of Nicodemus as he sees the broken body of the man he had once visited by night? Is he concerned mainly with the requirements of the Law regarding the burial or is he increasingly perplexed about the identity of Jesus? What thoughts does he confide to his friend Joseph during their ministrations?

Note: Though the details surrounding the regal burial of Jesus are to be interpreted theologically rather than historically, there is no reason why they should not be incorporated into the prayer of the Christian believer.

3. PRAYING WITH JESUS

We have no way of knowing whether Jesus met Nicodemus on more than one occasion. Our concern in this session is only with the night meeting and the impact it had on Jesus.

Having earlier prayed with the Pharisee and identified with him in his quest, we now enter imaginatively into the experience of Jesus himself. We accept his invitation, 'Remain here and keep watch with me' (Mt 26:38 // Mk 14:34), and join him as he addresses the God of Abraham, Isaac and Jacob in prayer.

This time we do not presume to pray in the first person. Instead, we listen as Jesus commends the struggling and perplexed Nicodemus to the loving care of his heavenly Father and as he reflects upon their encounter in the light of his growing awareness of his own saving mission. As stated in the Introduction, this is like sharing with Jesus the precious moments of his examination* of consciousness at the close of the day.

This is also a time for entering into our own dialogue with Jesus. However, we shall speak to him more fully about what is surfacing in our consciousness in the next session.

4. CONTEXTUAL PRAYER

Just as his meeting with Jesus was a revelatory event for Nicodemus, so also is our encounter with the Lord in the written account of it. Alive to the perennial relevance of Jesus' words to the Pharisee, we hear them and feel their impact in the context of our life here and now as they 'challenge [us] to be born again, to enter ever more fully into the mystery of divine revelation and thus to appropriate anew our identity as disciples' (Schneiders 1987a:196).

We alone know, in the uniqueness of our personal being, how these words resonate today in our life experience. This awareness forms the basis of our prayer in this session which is, as it were, the moment of truth for us. We acknowledge our failures, rejoice in the good that God's grace has been able to effect in us, and pray for the guidance and empowerment we need to live our Christian faith more authentically.

The reflections which follow are not intended to preempt the retreatant's own thoughts but to bring them into sharper focus. If they are unhelpful, ignore them.

Faith/discipleship. All divine revelation has its appropriate correlate in a faith response that identifies one as the

Day One

Lord's disciple. Resting on a sounder foundation than admiration of his signs, it is confessed and witnessed to publicly in holy fellowship with other believers.

As Nicodemus and the rich young ruler of the Lucan story (Lk 18:18-30) discover, this new covenant relationship with God is a pearl of great price (cf. Mt 13:45-46) 'costing not less than everything'. True disciples do not say, 'Yes, but ...' to God's offer of eternal life.

Setting aside every other consideration, they seek to be 'wise in Christ' (1 Cor 4:10), knowing the truth not merely as something to be contemplated but as something to be put into practice (2 Jn 4; 3 Jn 3). 'Whoever lives the truth', the evangelist assures us, 'comes to the light, so that his works may be clearly seen as done in God' (3:21).

Moreover, as Nicodemus learns in the meeting of the authorities (7:45-52), the follower of Jesus must be willing 'not only to believe in him but also to suffer for him' (Phil 1:29; cf. 2 Tim 3:12; Jn 15:20).

Conversion of heart. Although Nicodemus expects answers from Jesus, he receives only the ultimatum that he should be, in his own words, 'born again'. It is a call, compassionate but uncompromising, to conversion of heart — a call to die to himself so that he may be born anew to the fullness of life that Jesus has come to give (10:10; cf. 1:4; 3:16; 8:12; 10:28; 1 Jn 4:9; 5:11-12).

This is a challenge to which we ourselves must respond not in some once-and-for-all fashion but continually. It will always be difficult; for, as O'Day (1988:54) remarks:

> We are afraid to embrace newness, to accept transformation, because such acceptance would mean letting go of the things that defined our lives before newness was offered. We stubbornly cling to our definitions of life, because we are afraid to accept God's offer of a new identity.

Complacency. The main obstacle to on-going conversion for many of us may not be the weakness of spirit occasioned by habitual sin but a false sense of security flowing from the supercilious self-assurance with which we adhere to our religious position. We may vigorously maintain the orthodoxy of that stance and yet, at the same time, lack the freedom that should accompany the truth we profess. (cf. 8:32).

How easy it is to proclaim with confidence our membership of the household of the faith but overlook the fact that we are housed in the much-folded tent of a pilgrim people.

With good reason does Schneiders (1987a:194) invite us to reflect upon our openness to the word that God speaks to us today in the depths of our being by re-examining the underlying assumptions of religious commitment in the light of Nicodemus's meeting with Jesus:

> Nicodemus is not a figure of the past. He lives in the heart of every believer who is tempted to settle down in the secure religious 'wisdom' of the establishment and thus resist the challenge of on-going revelation.

Witness. For pastoral reasons associated with the pusillanimity of some members of his own faith community, the evangelist emphasises the fact that a willingness to witness publicly to Jesus is a *sine qua non* of true discipleship (cf. 1 Jn 1:1-3; 4:14).

We may be forced to admit to our shame and to our loss that we recognise ourselves in Cantwell's (1980:483) assessment of Nicodemus:

> The night enables Nicodemus to avoid committing himself, to keep his options and his bolt-holes open, to deceive himself into thinking that he can have some of the advantages of faith without paying the full price. The night hides Nicodemus not only from others but from himself.

Day One

Under this heading we might also give some thought to the courageous witness of some of our contemporaries living in oppressive regimes in different parts of the world where to claim a body for burial assumes the character of a political act. In all our contextual reflections throughout the retreat it is well to look not only at our own immediate concerns, pressing though they may be, but also at those of our neighbour.

5. PRAYING THE MANTRA

Finally, choose a brief sentence, a phrase, or even a single word from the scripture readings of the day which has special meaning to you at this moment, not in the sense that it conveys some profound thought but rather that it resonates in your being beyond the reach of thought.

Adopt a comfortable posture and chant your mantra at a suitable pitch (from your chest rather than from your throat) in keeping with the rhythm of your breathing. Let it gently vibrate within you as if you were but the instrument of the indwelling Spirit who prays for us 'with inexpressible groanings' (Rom 8:26).

If you have difficulty in selecting a mantra, these verses might provide a lead: 'God so loved the world that he gave his only Son' (3:16); 'Whoever lives the truth comes to the light' (3:21); 'Whoever believes in the Son has eternal life' (3:36).

DAY TWO

JESUS AND THE SAMARITAN WOMAN
(John 4:1-42)

1. REFLECTIVE STUDY OF THE TEXT

Introduction

> Oh, how often do I remember the living water of which the Lord spoke to the woman of Samaria! I am so fond of that Gospel. I have loved it ever since I was quite a child — though I did not, of course, understand it properly then, as I do now — and I often used to beseech the Lord to give me that water. I had a picture of the Lord at the well, which hung where I could always see it, and bore the inscription: 'Domine, da mihi aquam' (Teresa 1946:I,203).

In this reflection we direct our attention to the story of the Samaritan woman whose meeting with Jesus at Jacob's Well was, as the above extract from her autobiography indicates, a source of spiritual delight to St Teresa of Avila.

Let us begin this day of reflection by asking God, who 'knows the secrets of the heart' (Ps 44:21), for the living water of which Jesus speaks — the inestimable gift of his holy Spirit. We could conclude our prayer by making our own these words of the Psalmist (Ps 41:2-3 JB):

> Like the deer that yearns for running streams,
> so my soul is yearning for you, my God.

> My soul is thirsting for God, the God of my life;
> when can I enter and see the face of God?

Now read Jn 4:1-42 aloud, attentive to the words of Jesus which are addressed as much to the reader as to the original participants in this remarkable adventure in grace.

Preliminary observations

Unnamed and mentioned only by John, the Samaritan woman is a representative of the true Christian believer who, by acting as a herald of the Good News, brings others to believe in Jesus.

In focusing on her as a representative figure, however, we should not lose sight of the fact that she is an individual too, a unique human being like ourselves. As Cantwell (1983:73) reminds us: 'One major thing that is often missed by commentators is that any Gospel incident is not just a stage or facet in the exposition of Christ's message; it is also a moment in the life of a concrete human individual.'

This story is more likely to hit home to us if, keeping this observation in mind, we try to identify the various stages in the development of her faith in the one whom her people come to acknowledge as 'the savior of the world' (4:42).

Old Testament background

The Hebrew Scriptures record a number of encounters which take place at wells (see, for example, Gen 24). Indeed, several biblical characters meet their future wives in this manner. We may recall the meeting between Moses and the seven daughters of the priest of Midian, one of whom, Zipporah, is given to him in marriage (Ex 2:15-22).

However, of more immediate interest to us is the fact that Jacob woos Rachel, the daughter of Laban, at her

Day Two 105

father's well (Gen 29:1-14). It would be well to read this account before proceeding.

There are obvious similarities between Jesus' involvement with the Samaritan woman at Jacob's Well and the above-mentioned meetings. As Culpepper (1983:136) points out:

> The encounter takes place in a foreign land, the protagonist is expected to do or say something characteristic of his role in the story, one or other of them will draw water, and the maiden will rush home and prepare for the man's coming to meet her father and eat with them. A wedding will follow.

Because of their knowledge of these meeting texts in the Hebrew Scriptures, some at least of John's readers would have been quick to notice the subtle differences in his account of such a meeting.

Detailed commentary

Introduction (4:1-6)

> [1]Now when Jesus learned that the Pharisees had heard that Jesus was making and baptizing more disciples than John [2](although Jesus himself was not baptizing, just his disciples), [3]he left Judea and returned to Galilee. [4]He had to pass through Samaria. [5]So he came to a town of Samaria called Sychar, near the plot of land that Jacob had given to his son Joseph. [6]Jacob's well was there. Jesus, tired from his journey, sat down there at the well. It was about noon.

The evangelist begins the fourth chapter of his Gospel with a few transitional verses (4:1-3) which, with their references to baptism, link it thematically with the preceding incident in which Jesus confronts Nicodemus with the need to be born from above of water and Spirit (3:3-5). He then proceeds to set the scene for the encounter with the Samaritan woman by giving precise time and place indications (4:4-6).

The Pharisees, like the disciples of the Baptist (3:26), are concerned with the apparent success of Jesus' ministry. There are already signs of the popular acclaim for Jesus which will follow the raising of Lazarus and which will lead his enemies to say, 'Look, the whole world has gone after him' (12:19; cf. 11:48).

We are assured in one of the Gospel's many editorial asides (4:2) that Jesus himself (contrary to what is stated in 3:22) is content to leave baptismal activity to his disciples. The editor's purpose in making this assertion may be to bring this Gospel into line with the Synoptic writings.

The Pharisees, as Jesus doubtless knows, have already taken John the Baptist to task for baptising (1:24-25). Not wishing to court trouble and mindful of the fact that his hour has not yet come, Jesus wisely decides to leave Judea and return to Galilee. He will be safer there if we may judge by what is said in 7:1: 'After this, Jesus moved about within Galilee; but he did not wish to travel in Judea, because the Jews were trying to kill him.'

Geographically speaking, it was not necessary for Jesus to pass through Samaria in order to reach Galilee. Many Jews, because of enmity between them and the Samaritans, preferred to take the more easterly route along the Jordan valley even though it was hotter and rather more difficult. This was especially the case when they were travelling south to Jerusalem for the Temple festivals. We know from Mark's Gospel that Jesus had occasion to use this Transjordanian detour (Mk 10:1).

The statement that Jesus 'had to pass through Samaria' (4:4) is best understood as indicating some sense of urgency in his mission derived from his understanding of and fidelity to God's will. He must do the works of the one who sent him (9:4).[1]

Scholars debate the location of the town of Sychar. From early times it has been identified (by St Jerome among others) with Schechem which is probably the present day village of Askar, about 800 metres to the northeast of the Jacob's Well visited by pilgrims to the Holy Land.

Without mentioning that there was a well in that place, Genesis 48:22 (cf. Gen 33:18-19) records that the patriarch Jacob gave Schechem to his son Joseph, 'the one above his brothers'. The bones of Joseph, which the Israelites had brought up from Egypt, were eventually buried there (Josh 24:32).

Tired from his journey and in need of refreshment, Jesus, the son of another Joseph (1:45; 6:42), sits down by the town well of Sychar (Schechem); and the scene is set for one of the most dramatic encounters in the four Gospels. With characteristic attention to detail, John tells us that 'it was about noon' (4:6).

As Lightfoot (1960:122) points out, this same phrase is used again in the account of Jesus' passion (19:14) just before he is handed over to be crucified as 'the savior of the world'. It is one of a number of echoes of the passion narrative to be found in this chapter.

Scene 1 (4:7-26)

(a) The meeting with the Samaritan woman (4:7-9)

⁷A woman of Samaria came to draw water. Jesus said to her, 'Give me a drink.' ⁸His disciples had gone into

---

[1] For all that, we may note that Samaria does not seem to loom largely in Jesus' missionary priorities. It is not mentioned in Mark; the Twelve are told to avoid it in Matthew (Mt 10:5-6; cf. 15:24); and Jesus ministers there with conspicuous lack of success in Luke only en route to Jerusalem (Lk 9:51-56; 17:11).

the town to buy food. ⁹The Samaritan woman said to him, 'How can you, a Jew, ask me, a Samaritan woman, for a drink?' (For Jews use nothing in common with Samaritans.)

As he so often does in the Fourth Gospel, Jesus takes the initiative. He begins the longest conversation he has with anyone in the whole four Gospels by asking an anonymous Samaritan woman for a drink (cf. 19:28). She has come to draw water from the local well. For some reason (is it to avoid people?) she has come at noon in the heat of the day instead of at the more usual time 'near evening ... when women go out to draw water' (Gen 24:11; cf. 29:7).

Jesus' contemporaries (his own disciples among them) would have been astounded by his laxity in speaking with one who, in Letty Russell's (1982:24) pithy phrase is 'foreign, fallen, and female!' It was not customary for a man to speak to an unaccompanied woman, the more so if she were known to be an enemy and thought to be a sinner.[2]

Jesus' critics might well have recalled for him these pertinent words of Sirach:
> My whole being loathes two nations,
> the third is not even a people:
> Those who live in Seir and Philistia,
> and the degenerate folk who dwell in Schechem
> (Sir 50: 25-26).

For his part, Jesus is more content to anticipate in practice what Paul was to write to the Galatians:

---

[2] It appears that the evangelist presents the woman as a sinner. However, it may be that she has fallen from favour rather than from grace. In the eyes of the Jews (Jesus' own disciples among them) the mere fact that she is a Samaritan is sufficient to label her as a sinner, regardless of the interpretation they might be disposed to place on her relationships with men.

Day Two

> There is neither Jew nor Greek, there is neither slave nor free person, there is not male and female; for you are all one in Christ Jesus. And if you belong to Christ, then you are Abraham's descendant, heirs according to the promise (Gal 3:28-29; cf. Rom 15:7-12).

It is especially noteworthy that Jesus is never condescending in his approach to the Samaritan woman or, for that matter, to any other woman.[3] Indeed, as the story unfolds, he goes a long way towards restoring her lost self-respect. At a time when some rabbis considered it sinful to teach a woman the Law*, he is happy to share with her wisdom which far surpasses that of Solomon (cf. Mt 12:42 // Lk 11:31), wisdom which, in a unique sense, is 'a fountain of life' (Prov 13:14; 16:22), 'a flowing brook' (Prov 18:4).

That being said, we should not overlook the fact that what takes place between Jesus and the unnamed woman of Samaria is a genuine dialogue. She has her own contribution to make; and Jesus is open to receive it.

In keeping with the dramatic 'rule of two', the evangelist sees to it that the disciples are off the scene when the dialogue between Jesus and the woman takes place. Of course, this may well be an historically accurate detail, in which case we may surmise how they are faring in their dealings with the townspeople (cf. Lk 9:51-56).

Not surprisingly, the woman's response to Jesus' request is one of amazement that he, whose appearance betrays the fact that he is a Jew, should ask a favour of a Samaritan woman. Was he not of that race which spoke of Samaritan women as 'menstrous [and, therefore, unclean] from birth' (cf. Lev 15:19)? As the editorial comment in 4:9 implies,

---

[3] On the radical nature of Jesus' relationships with women generally, see Grenier (1984).

it was unthinkable for a Jew to drink from a vessel contaminated by the touch of someone ritually impure, as all Samaritans were considered to be. This would render one unfit to take part in worship just as effectively as if one had made contact with a corpse (cf. Num 19:11-22).

Like that of Nathanael (1:46), the woman's relationship with Jesus can hardly be said to have had an auspicious beginning, in spite of Cantwell's (1983:80) observation that her remark expresses more 'the indignation of self-depreciation than of arrogance'. She calls him a 'Jew' with hardly more warmth, we may suppose, than his own people describe him as a 'Samaritan' (8:48).

Having noted that, in the original story, the issue was the relationship between the Jews and the Samaritans in Jesus' day, we may look for an underlying pastoral intention in the evangelist's writing. In the early Christian Church the issue was probably friction arising from the relationship between Jewish Christians and Samaritan Christians (cf. Acts 8:4-25).

(b) The discourse on living water (4:10-15)

[10]Jesus answered and said to her, 'If you knew the gift of God and who is saying to you, "Give me a drink," you would have asked him and he would have given you living water.' [11][The woman] said to him, 'Sir, you do not even have a bucket and the cistern is deep; where can you get this living water? [12]Are you greater than our father Jacob, who gave us this cistern and drank from it himself with his children and his flocks?' [13]Jesus answered and said to her, 'Everyone who drinks this water will be thirsty again; [14]but whoever drinks the water I shall give will never thirst; the water I shall give will become in him a spring of water welling up to eternal life.' [15]The woman said to him, 'Sir, give me this water, so that I may not be thirsty or have to keep coming here to draw water.'

Day Two

The preliminaries over, Jesus 'elevates' the conversation by introducing the theme of a significant discourse — a word of revelation not only for the Samaritan woman but for us too. Doubtless, the evangelist's original readers would have appreciated the sacramental allusion in the phrase 'living water' which recalls the water/spirit discussion that Jesus had with Nicodemus (3:3-8).

Indeed, as Lightfoot (1960:121) illustrates, 'the theme of water runs like a silver thread through the early chapters of this gospel'; and Tertullian, speaking more generally in his *Treatise on Baptism*, states:

> Never does Christ appear without water. He was himself baptised in it. It was through water that he showed the first sign of his divine power at the marriage feast. In his preaching he called all who thirst to the water of eternal life. When he spoke of love, he numbered among the works of charity the giving of a cup of cold water to one's neighbour. He recruited his strength by resting beside a well. He walked on water, freely crossed the sea, washed the feet of his disciples with water. And water continued to bear witness even in his Passion. When he was condemned to the cross, water played its part, as Pilate's hands can testify; and when he was pierced by the soldier's lance, water gushed forth from his side (Ashworth 1973:126-27).

The 'living water' theme is taken up again in Jesus' address on the last day of the Festival of Tabernacles* (7:37-39). In this instance, in an explanatory aside, John identifies the 'living water' (and, therefore, the gift which Jesus has to offer) with the Spirit (cf. Acts 2:38; 8:18-20; 10:45; 11:17; Heb 6:4).

This is a gift which Jesus himself possesses without measure. 'For the one whom God sent speaks the words of God. He does not ration his gift of the Spirit. The Father loves the Son and has given everything over to him' (3:34-35; cf. 16:15).

In another context, in a verse which sums up the entire Gospel, the evangelist identifies Jesus himself as God's gift: 'For God so loved the world that he gave his only Son, so that everyone who believes in him might not perish but might have eternal life' (3:16).

To speak of 'living water' is to identify water that flows from some source like a spring rather than the sometimes unpalatable, even stagnant, water that may be found in a well. In a country where it rarely rains between May and October, such discourse would inevitably strike a responsive chord in people (the Samaritan woman among them) for whom water was a much prized commodity (cf. Ezek 47:112; Zech 14:8).

It suggested paradise to the Jews (cf. 1 Enoch 22:9) and symbolised for them the future prosperity of Zion (see Is 30:23-26; 41:17-18; 43:19-20; 44:3-4; 49:10) just as, for the early Christians, it became a symbol or promise related to the final state of salvation when the Lamb would 'lead them to springs of life-giving water' (Rev 7:17; cf. Ps 23:2; 36:9)

But let us return to the woman who is drinking in what Jesus has to say. At first she appears to be in control of the situation. After all, she has a water jar (4:28) and is probably surprised that Jesus does not have the skin 'bucket' that travellers usually carry for such emergencies. However, as she will learn and as we well know, Jesus is always the one in control in the Fourth Gospel.

Seemingly a practical and down-to-earth person, the Samaritan misunderstands Jesus' words. Thinking that he is speaking literally when he offers her 'living water', she concludes that he has access to a special and not generally known source.

Although she fails to comprehend Jesus' offer, she is much more receptive than Nicodemus and 'the Jews'

Day Two

generally (as John portrays them);[4] and she actually asks him for this precious gift. Her misunderstanding is more like that of the disciples (cf. 4:31-38); it is inadequate rather than perverse. She has yet to appreciate that Jesus' gifts are 'from above' (3:3; 6:31-33) just as Jesus himself is (7:27-29; 8:14; 9:29-30; 19:9).

Addressing him politely as 'Sir', she enquires with delightful irony, 'Are you greater than our father Jacob ...?' Like the Jews who will ask Jesus, 'Are you greater than our father Abraham, who died?' (8:53), the Samaritans held the patriarchs in high esteem.

Pointedly, Neyrey (1979:420-21) observes:
> Together the two questions belong to a theme in the Gospel which asserts Jesus' superiority to the founding fathers of traditional Jewish religion (see 1:17-18; 5:38; 6:32). The thrust of the question, as we shall see, suggests that Jesus not only replaces Jacob, Abraham, and Moses vis-à-vis God's revelation, but that an absolute claim is made on his behalf: he is *greater* than these, he supplants them with new revelation, a new cult and a new covenant.

Just as Jacob supplanted his brother Esau (Gen 25:24-26 — birth; 25:30-34 — birthright; 27:36 — blessing), so also is Jacob himself supplanted by Jesus. We may note, in passing, how common this theme of supplanting is in folk literature in general and in the Hebrew Scriptures in particular.

In similar vein, in a number of antithetical statements which highlight his superiority (or absolute importance), we are told that Jesus is the 'true light' (1:9), the 'true bread from heaven' (6:32), and the 'true vine' (15:1).

---

4 The qualification, 'as John portrays them', is a necessary one because his Gospel reflects the mutual antipathy of Jews and Christians at the time of its composition. More will be said in this connection when we come to consider the story of the man born blind.

Moreover, as he tells the Samaritan woman (4:13-14), the water that he alone has to offer will satisfy the deepest of all human longings more effectively than the personified Wisdom his forebears extolled and of whom Sirach wrote: 'He who drinks of me will thirst for more' (Sir 24:20).

Her eager response calls to mind the request of the Jews on another occasion: 'Sir, give us this bread always' (6:34); but it reveals a like misunderstanding of what Jesus has in mind. Her hope is that the gift the Galilean speaks of will deliver her from the necessity of these daily trips to the well which are such a tedious and burdensome chore for the women of the village and (presuming that she is regarded as a sinner) a painful reminder of her social ostracism.

(c) The woman's life disclosed (4:16-19)

> [16]Jesus said to her, 'Go call your husband and come back.' [17]The woman answered and said to him, 'I do not have a husband.' Jesus answered her, 'You are right in saying, "I do not have a husband." [18]For you have had five husbands, and the one you have now is not your husband. What you have said is true.' [19]The woman said to him, 'Sir, I can see that you are a prophet.'

At this point in the story, again on Jesus' initiative, there is an abrupt transition. The woman's request for 'living water' is not ignored but is set aside so that her real thirst may be revealed to her (cf. Ps 42:1-3). 'A man of intelligence', he is able to draw forth 'the intention in the human heart [which] is like water far below the surface' (Prov 20:5).

The fact that Jesus displays more than human knowledge in doing so is fully consistent with the Johannine portrait of the God-Man. John tells us that '[Jesus] did not need anyone to testify about human nature. He himself understood it well' (2:25).[5]

It may be that Jesus is expressing his compassion for the woman who, more than likely, has been abused by men and who is more sinned against than sinning. In any case, he is not so much concerned with getting her to abandon her sinful ways, if such they be, as he is with making her receptive to his revelation. If there is need for change, she will change in due course. In the meantime, as Cantwell (1983:80) puts it, 'There is in her neither the splendour of virtue nor the fascination of vice.'

What may be significant, especially given the evangelist's penchant for grouping things in sevens (a number suggestive of completeness or perfection), is the fact that Jesus himself is the seventh man in her presumably rather unhappy life. With him come new possibilities of personal fulfilment.[6]

More than the woman's curiosity is aroused by Jesus' insight; she is also growing slowly towards a position of faith in him. As Jesus reveals himself to her more fully, we will observe a progression in the titles she employs:

---

[5] Some interpreters see in Jesus' reference to 'five husbands' an allusion to the five idolatrous cults that the Samaritans embraced after the Assyrians overran the northern kingdom in 722 B.C.E. (2 Kings 17:24,30-31). The discussion on true worship in 4:20-24 could lend weight to this suggestion, the more so as idolatry was often equated with adultery in the Hebrew Scriptures (cf. Neh 13:23-31). However, the fact that she calls Jesus a prophet (4:19) weakens the allegorical interpretation. A literal reading, which construes Jesus' judgment (if indeed it is a judgment) in personal ethical terms rather than in collective allegorical terms, would make the Samaritan's statement to her townspeople more comprehensible: 'Come see a man who told me everything I have done' (4:29).

[6] Perhaps, in reflecting on these verses, we would do well to consider other matrimonial references in the Fourth Gospel. Taking account of 2:1-11 (Cana), 3:29 (the Baptist's witness about the groom and the best man), and 4:18, Neyrey (1979:426) remarks: 'Thus in matrimonial imagery Jesus has been proclaimed as winning the allegiance of new followers and as supplanting previous persons and rituals in Jewish religion.'

'Jew' (4:9), 'Sir' (4:11,19), 'prophet' (4:19), 'Messiah' (4:29). There is a similar progression in the narrative of the cure of the man born blind who also identifies Jesus as a prophet (9:17).

'Prophet', we may add in passing, is a title which the woman herself richly deserves. Perhaps it takes a prophet to recognise one.

(d) The discourse on true worship (4:20-24)

> [20]'Our ancestors worshiped on this mountain; but you people say that the place to worship is in Jerusalem.' [21]Jesus said to her, 'Believe me, woman, the hour is coming when you will worship the Father neither on this mountain nor in Jerusalem. [22]You people worship what you do not understand; we worship what we understand, because salvation is from the Jews. [23]But the hour is coming, and is now here, when true worshipers will worship the Father in Spirit and truth; and indeed the Father seeks such people to worship him. [24]God is Spirit, and those who worship him must worship in Spirit and truth.'

This time it is the woman who changes the direction of the dialogue by raising a question which was the source of much acrimonious debate between the Jews and the Samaritans. Some commentators have suggested that she does so in order to take the attention away from her own personal life; but it may be simpler to interpret her remark as a mild reproof, implying that Jesus should concern himself with more important issues. In any event, the writer contrives to provide Jesus with the cue he needs to speak about the nature of true worship.

The traditional place associated with Samaritan worship is Mt Gerazim which dominates the scene even as Jesus and the woman converse. In the Samaritan Pentateuch* (contrary to what is stated in the Hebrew Scriptures), it

Day Two

was on this mountain rather than on the adjacent Mt Ebal that the Israelites, at God's command, built an altar after their entry into the Promised Land (see Deut 27:4-8,11-13; cf. 11:29; Josh 8:33). Both Abraham (Gen 12:6-7) and Jacob (Gen 33:18-20) had also constructed altars nearby.

The Samaritans came to erect their own temple there when the Jews, after their return from exile in Babylon, excluded them from worship in the rebuilt Temple of the Lord in Jerusalem. Built by Manasseh, a renegade Jew who had married the daughter of Sanballat the Horonite, the governor of Samaria, this Samaritan temple was destroyed by John Hyrcanus (135-104 B.C.E.) during the time of the Maccabees. From that time the enmity between the two peoples became ever more virulent. (For fuller details, consult the Books of Ezra and Nehemiah).

The woman wants a 'yes' or 'no' answer to her question. In the light of Deut 12:1-14, which Hyrcanus might well have invoked in his mission of destruction, there can be only one true temple erected to the Lord.

The point that Jesus makes is that her question and the long-standing argument between the Jews and the Samaritans are no longer relevant. He himself is the new Temple, as he proclaimed when he cleansed the Temple in Jerusalem on the occasion of the first Passover feast mentioned in John (2:13-22). True worship, from this time onwards, transcends and is independent of all previously sanctioned holy places (cf. Acts 17:24).

This truth is made abundantly clear in the apocalyptic* description of the New Jerusalem in the Book of Revelation: 'I saw no temple in the city, for its temple is the Lord God almighty and the Lamb' (Rev 21:22).

No doubt the evangelist, in his pastoral zeal, hoped to develop this awareness in his community; for it is not unlikely that some residual antipathy remained amongst

Christians who still cherished either their Jewish or their Samaritan backgrounds.

We should note, because it is germane to the above discussion, that the Samaritan Christians had to face an added problem. Since their people recognised only the Pentateuch, both their theology and their worship (without the Psalms!) were impoverished.

Deferential, as always in his dealings with women, Jesus addresses his interlocutor as 'woman' (cf. 2:4; 19:26 — his mother; 20:13,15 — Mary Magdalen). He assures her, in language which is typically Johannine (cf. 4:23; 5:25,28; 16:2,25,32): 'The hour is coming when you will worship the Father neither on this mountain nor in Jerusalem' (4:21). True worshipers in the new dispensation will worship the Father in 'Spirit and truth'.

Commentators are not in agreement about the meaning of this phrase. As well as pointing to the need for inner dispositions appropriate to the intimate act of worshiping a loving Father, it seems to indicate that we are not empowered to worship a transcendent God authentically until we have been transformed by God's holy Spirit. In Jesus' words to Nicodemus, we must be reborn from above (3:3).

This having been said, Jesus takes the dialogue a step further by informing the Samaritan woman, in a gently uncompromising way, that 'salvation is from the Jews' (4:22). In this statement (it is the only time the word 'salvation' is used in John), Jesus is not simply giving voice to nationalistic sentiment. He is speaking of the advent of the Messiah who will assuredly not be a Samaritan (cf. Lk 1:69,71,77; Acts 4:12; 13:26,46-47).

(e) *The revelation of Jesus as the Messiah (4:25-26)*

> 25The woman said to him, 'I know that the Messiah is coming, the one called the Anointed; when he comes,

he will tell us everything.' ²⁶Jesus said to her, 'I am he, the one who is speaking with you.'

The woman is not put out by Jesus' assertion concerning salvation; and she continues to stand up for her religion. However, the terminology attributed to her by the evangelist is Jewish rather than Samaritan (cf. 4:29). Having only the Pentateuch to guide them, it was not a messianic king of the house of David whom her people awaited but a prophet like Moses (Deut 18:15-18). They referred to this rather politicised figure, who would restore the Kingdom of Israel and, with it, true worship, as the *taheb*, 'the one who returns'. He was the object of the woman's hope until the *kairos** moment of her meeting with Jesus.

Her talk of the Messiah (cf. Jesus' own words in 16:13) sets the scene for Jesus to declare who he is. It is characteristic of him to reveal himself more fully when anyone, open to his word, responds to him in faith (cf. 9:37). 'I am he, the one who is speaking to you,' he says.

We are not told how she reacts to this disclosure. The Fourth Gospel does not dwell on such matters.

Scene 2 (4:27-38)

(a) Introduction (4:27-30)

²⁷At that moment his disciples returned, and were amazed that he was talking with a woman, but still no one said, 'What are you looking for?' or 'Why are you talking with her?' ²⁸The woman left her water jar and went into the town and said to the people, ²⁹'Come see a man who told me everything I have done. Could he possibly be the Messiah?' ³⁰They went out of the town and came to him.

In the light of our earlier comments, it should be obvious why the disciples, on their return from the town, are surprised to find Jesus talking with a woman. As yet, they do not understand the nature of his saving mission; and, mindful of his enigmatic behaviour on other occasions, they have the good sense not to question him (cf. 21:12).

The woman, on the other hand, anxious to share her experience with her friends (including, presumably, 'husband' number six), leaves her water jar behind and makes for the town. The jar, as Flanagan (1981:266) felicitously puts it, is 'a stage whisper that the Samaritan woman will return'.

In passing, it is interesting to note that the only other place in the New Testament where the Greek word for a water jar is used is in John's account of the wedding feast at Cana.

With courage worthy of the disciples after Pentecost, the woman witnesses publicly and compellingly to what she has seen and heard. A missionary of salvation to her own people (cf. 3:17), she calls others to Jesus in words which recall his own invitation to the two followers of the Baptist (1:39).

Their curiosity aroused, they seek Jesus out. They might well have said what other non-Jews will say to Philip, 'We would like to see Jesus' (12:21).

(b) The discourse on mission (4:31-38)

31Meanwhile, the disciples urged him, 'Rabbi, eat.' 32But he said to them, 'I have food to eat of which you do not know.' 33So the disciples said to one another, 'Could someone have brought him something to eat?' 34Jesus said to them, 'My food is to do the will of the one who sent me and to finish his work. 35Do you not say, "In four months the harvest will be here"? I tell you, look up and see the fields ripe for the harvest. 36The reaper is already receiving his payment and gathering crops for eternal life, so that the sower and reaper can rejoice together. ³⁷For here the saying is verified that "One sows and another reaps." ³⁸I sent you to reap what you have not worked for; others have done the work, and you are sharing the fruits of their work.'

The disciples, their food-gathering mission completed, urge Jesus to eat. Thus they (or should we say the writer) provide him with the cue he needs to launch into yet another discourse. He begins by telling them, 'I have food to eat of which you do not know.'

Needless to say, they do not comprehend what he means. Taking his words literally and questioning one another rather than Jesus himself directly (cf. 4:27; 21:12), they conjecture as to whether someone may have provided him with food in their absence. Their misunderstanding concerning food parallels the woman's misunderstanding concerning drink.

By way of clarification, Jesus adds: 'My food is to do the will of the one who sent me and to finish his work.' It is time for them to learn something about his mission — the mission he was exercising while they were in the town when, as always, he was doing his Father's work. Only on the cross will he be able to say, 'It is finished' (19:30; cf. 17:4).

After his resurrection, Jesus will say to his disciples, 'As the Father has sent me, so I send you' (20:21; cf. 17:18; 13:15-16). They too will have work to do in his name and in the strength of his spirit; for the Christian Church is essentially a community in mission.

The nature of their task is implied in the proverb which Jesus quotes: 'In four months the harvest will be here.' 'Fishers of men' in the language of the Synoptic Gospels (Mt 4:19 // Mk 1:17; cf. Lk 5:10), they are to become, in Johannine imagery, the reapers of a rich harvest of souls (cf. Mt 9:37-38 // Lk 10:2; see also Mk 4:26-29).

The harvest usually began at the end of April. However, there is no need to wait for four months for the fruit of Jesus' sowing. Even as he is speaking to his disciples, a group of Samaritans is crossing the field and coming towards them. Perhaps Jesus gestures towards the townspeople as he says, 'Look up and see the fields ripe for the harvest.' According to Schnackenburg (1968:448), 'This present success is seen by Jesus as a highly promising sign for the future mission.'

Given the context of people's coming to a position of faith, Jesus' talk of 'gathering crops for eternal life' is quite appropriate.

Normally the reaper was paid at the end of the day's work, months after the sower had received his due; but, in the case of the work that Jesus does in his Father's name, both 'the sower [the Father] and reaper [Jesus] can rejoice together' (cf. Ps 126:5-6).

In Schnackenburg's (1968:45) words: 'Jesus's "reward" is simply the joy of harvest (36c); his life and his work are so clearly identified (v.34) that his only desire is to see the "harvest".'

In the immediate context, one might also say that the woman, who models a true disciple's missionary behaviour, is an extraordinarily effective sower with respect to her own people and that Jesus is the reaper.

Jesus concludes his discourse (these are his last words in the narrative) by saying: 'I sent you to reap what you have not worked for; others have done the work, and you are sharing the fruits of their work.' If we take this remark as referring to the later missionary experience of Christ's followers, 'others' may refer to Jesus himself; but it could also refer to the Samaritan woman and to women and men like her who evangelised Samaria in the early Church (Acts 8:4-17 — Philip sowed and Peter and John reaped).

Scene 3 (4:39-42)

> ³⁹Many of the Samaritans in that town began to believe in him because of the word of the woman who testified, 'He told me everything I have done.' ⁴⁰When the Samaritans came to him, they invited him to stay with them; and he stayed there two days. ⁴¹Many more came to believe in him because of his word, ⁴²and they said to the woman, 'We no longer believe because of your word; for we have heard for ourselves, and we know that this is truly the savior of the world.'

The concluding verses record the conversion of the Samaritan people in Schechem. Clearly the woman's testimony has borne fruit; like the Baptist (1:35-37), Andrew (1:40-42) and Philip (1:45-50), she has succeeded in leading others to Jesus. Their faith becomes stronger when they meet Jesus and hear him for themselves.

Note that the townspeople impose on Jesus to stay with them. Nowhere in the Gospels does he force himself upon people; for authentic faith is always characterised by freedom (cf. 6:66-67; Lk 24:29).

We can only surmise where Jesus and his disciples dwell during the two days they remain. Perhaps he stays with the woman and her 'husband' while his companions are billeted out. In any event, it is a remarkable occurrence — a group of Jews enjoying the hospitality of Samaritans — which must surely test the religious sensibilities of Jesus' disciples. In particular, we might wonder how Judas, the Judean, feels.

There is more to the word 'stayed' (*menein* in Greek) than at first meets the eye. In Johannine theology it commonly denotes the intimate and very special kind of presence (cf. 15:4-7,10) which is conveyed by the English word 'abide'. As O'Day (1986:87) expresses it:

> 'To dwell' with Jesus is to have direct contact with him, to share in his relationship with God. The note with which

v. 40 concludes, therefore, is not just an incidental narrative but an important commentary on Jesus' relationship with the Samaritans.

We are not told what Jesus says to the Samaritans. All we know is that his words, heavenly in their origin (3:34; 7:16; 12:49, 14:10; 17:6,8,14,17), are abundantly fruitful. For them they are 'spirit and life' (6:63).

The writer is at pains to contrast the Samaritans' faith with the lack of faith of 'the Jews' (see 1:11; 4:1-3,44; 6:30-31,41,52) who have forsaken 'the source of living waters' (Jer 2:13; 17:13) and to whom Jesus says in judgment: 'Whoever belongs to God hears the words of God; for this reason you do not listen, because you do not belong to God' (8:47; cf. 18:37). Truly, 'salvation is from the Jews' (4:22); but ironically it is accepted by the Samaritans.

The title, 'savior of the world', which is peculiar to John among the Gospels (cf. 1 Jn 4:14), climaxes the titles accorded to Jesus in this story. It is a title very much in keeping with Johannine Christology* which is fundamentally soteriological* (that is, focusing on the saving character of Jesus' mission). Moreover, it is essentially a Christian title (cf. Acts 5:31; 13:23; Phil 3:20); it was not in use for the Messiah in Judaism.

In faith we affirm that Jesus is a saviour who surpassed the messianic expectations of the Jews and the Samaritans alike (cf. Lk 24). 'There is no salvation through anyone else, nor is there any other name under heaven given to the human race by which we are to be saved' (Acts 4:12).

So much for our commentary on the text. Hopefully, it meets with the approval of the Samaritan woman of whom Cantwell (1983:73) writes:

> From those high fountains where now she drinks her fill of the waters of life the woman of Samaria may permit herself a wry smile at the curiously contorted ways in which some of her modern commentators re-tell her story.

2. IMAGINATIVE PRAYER WITH THE SAMARITAN WOMAN

Begin by spending some time with the Samaritan woman and her live-in lover in their home in Sychar. Be conscious of the heat of the day as, towards noon, she lifts a water jar on her head and walks the much-travelled path to the well outside the town. Even before it is filled with water, the jar is heavy with the burden of living as a woman in a patriarchal society. What are her thoughts as she makes this tediously familiar journey? What is her reaction when she sees in the distance a lone man seated by the well?

Stand in her shoes and play out her encounter with the Galilean intruder until that point when she returns to acquaint her townspeople of the remarkable things that Jesus has said to her. Trace (by experiencing it) the gradual change in her attitude towards him. What is her emotional response to Jesus' observations about her intimate relationships? What is it about Jesus that inspires confidence in her?

Make the hasty journey back to the town with her, unencumbered not only by the water jar but also by the burdens of life that have weighed so heavily upon her for years. What is she thinking as she approaches her home to share her experience with the man whom Jesus has asked to see? Listen as she excitedly relates her story to him and to her neighbours. How do they react to what she tells them?

Accompany her as she and her townspeople (are there any dissenters?) welcome Jesus to Sychar. Does he accept her offer of hospitality during his sojourn among them? How are Jesus' disciples coping with this extraordinary turn of events? What further words does Jesus direct to the Samaritan woman and her 'husband'?

What passes through her mind on the days following the visit of Jesus as she makes her way to draw water at the well? How does she feel about herself?

3. PRAYING WITH JESUS

In his sermon on the mount Jesus gives his disciples (ourselves included) some sound advice on how to pray (Mt 6:5-15; cf. Lk 11:1-4). Among other things he says: 'But when you pray, go to your inner room, close the door, and pray to your Father in secret' (Mt 6:6).

Let us now join Jesus as he himself, on his last evening in the Samaritan village, retires to a place where he can commune with his heavenly Father. With strong emotions he recalls the events of the past few days: the first moments of his meeting with the woman, the conversation with her which has borne such abundant fruit, the incomprehension of his disciples, the acknowledgement he has received from such an unlikely quarter.

We attend with reverence as he pours his heart out to the one who sent him and whose work he must finish (4:34).

Finally, we repeat the request of one of his disciples and say, 'Lord, teach us to pray' (Lk 11:1); and we listen to the words that he addresses here and now uniquely to us.

4. PRAYING CONTEXTUALLY

This is not a time for determining in a detached manner the possible relevance of the passage under consideration to the lives of contemporary Christians in general. Rather, it is a time for personal prayer, the focus of which is the agenda that has surfaced for oneself as a consequence of the earlier sessions.

This agenda may relate to a variety of issues of which one has personal experience: prejudice in any of its many ugly forms (racial, religious, ethnic, ...), the continuing oppression of women in Church and society today, judgmental and self-righteous attitudes towards sinners, marriage problems, or a poor self-image stemming from any of the aforementioned.

Please weigh up the immediate usefulness of what follows in the light of your own agenda. However, given the special importance of the theme of mission in today's reading, it would be well to return to this material later if it is not used now as the basis of contextual prayer.

Mission. The theme of mission — 'the organising principle of the message of the Fourth Gospel', in Comblin's (1979:vii) judgment — is unquestionably central to the evangelist's account of Jesus' meeting with the Samaritan woman and the people of Sychar. It is a sense of missionary urgency that leads him through the heartland of a hostile province; and it is about mission fields 'ripe for the harvest' (4:35) that he speaks to his chosen ones.

Moreover, we are confronted with the challenging example of the woman herself in this regard. Even before her faith in Jesus has matured to the point of total commitment, she acts in a manner befitting a disciple. Concerned to share with others the liberating experience she has enjoyed, she invites her townspeople to meet a man whom she believes, albeit tentatively, could be the long-awaited Messiah (4:29).

Her courage might prompt us to ask ourselves whether we have even begun to take seriously our call as Christians to spread the Good News with missionary zeal. Have we heard as a personal commission Jesus' words, 'As the Father has sent me, so I send you' (20:21; cf. 17:18)?

To clarify the nature of this call, note briefly some key elements of the Johannine teaching on the mission of Jesus, the divine origin of which is affirmed more than forty times in the Gospel.

Jesus' mission is of cosmic dimensions; for he is the Father's gift (cf. 3:16) not only to the House of Israel but to the whole world. The Baptist acclaims him as 'the Lamb of God, who takes away the sin *of the world*' (1:29); the Samaritans, as we have seen, confess him as 'truly the savior *of the world*' (4:42); and Jesus speaks of himself as 'the living bread ... for the life *of the world*' (6:51) and as 'the light *of the world*' (8:12; 9:5; cf. 1:4; 12:46).

He is more than just the last in the long line of witnesses whom God called to be his envoys and agents from the time of Moses onwards (cf. Heb 1:1-2). Both the messenger and the message, Jesus is the plenipotentiary on whom 'the Father, God, has set his seal' (6:27; 3:33). He is the creative, revealing, saving Word made flesh (cf. 1:14).

If Jesus' mission defines him, it also defines the mission of his disciples. We too, empowered by his Spirit (cf. 15:26-27) in virtue of our baptism and confirmation, are to proclaim the saving truth with its promise of fullness of life (cf. 10:10; 1 Jn 4:9). His words must become our words as we endeavour to do always what is pleasing to God (cf. 8:29): 'My food is to do the will of the one who sent me and to finish his work' (4:34).

5. PRAYING THE MANTRA

To assist yourself in the choice of a mantra (always a very personal matter), pause for a moment or two and ask yourself what text has spoken to you most insistently today or what word of scripture most clearly expresses what you want to say to God at this time. It may give voice to your pain and confusion, to some deeply felt need, to a heartfelt desire to praise and thank God for graces received, to great joy in the loving presence of God, to sorrow for sin, to concern for the well-being of others, et cetera. In any case, the longer you pray the mantra the less important the chosen words become.

A few texts (adapted to suit) that commend themselves to me include: 'Lord, give me this living water' (cf. 4:15); 'You are truly the savior of the world' (cf. 4:42); or simply, 'the gift of God' (cf. 4:10).

DAY THREE

JESUS AND THE MAN BORN BLIND
(John 9:1-41)

1. REFLECTIVE STUDY OF THE TEXT

Introduction

We need to remind ourselves at the beginning of each day of our retreat that the time devoted to serious study of the sacred text is not merely an academic exercise designed to prepare us for the 'real' prayer sessions that follow later in the day. It is itself a prayer if, conscious of God's presence to us in the scriptural word, we study it not for the sake of adding to the store of our human knowledge but 'to know the love of Christ that surpasses knowledge, so that [we] may be filled with all the fullness of God' (Eph 3:19).

Our chosen passage for today is the story of the man born blind — one of the many stories in the Gospels which we can return to time and time again not only for the added insights they yield about the people who encountered Jesus but also for the light they cast on our own faith journey.

By way of preparation, spend a few quiet moments in prayer. You may like to conclude with these words of St Augustine (1961:279):

> O Lord my God, how deep are your mysteries! How far from your safe haven have I been cast away by the

consequences of my sins! Heal my eyes and let me rejoice in your light.

Now read Jn 9:1-41 aloud, savouring the drama of the situation. A second reading will be called for at appropriate places in the detailed commentary below.

Preliminary observations

Historical context

The commentary takes the narrative as it stands. It acknowledges, therefore, the perspective of the evangelist; but, at the same time, it is critical of that necessarily limited point of view, conditioned as it was both by historical circumstances and by the pastoral needs of the Johannine church. These remarks are, as we will see, especially pertinent to John's portrayal of the Pharisees.

We should not lose sight of the fact that the Christian Gospels were being written at a time when important changes were taking place within Judaism in response to the Roman domination. These changes reflected not only markedly different stances with respect to the political situation but also divergent schools of thought (some progressive, others conservative) within the Jewish religious community itself.

At such a time of uncertainty and instability, the authentic Jewish leadership understandably viewed with suspicion and countered with vigour anything which might have threatened the identity and unity of the people. Not surprisingly, the early Christians, followers of one whom they revered as the long-awaited Messiah of Israel, found themselves at odds with some of their neighbours and, more particularly, with the religious establishment.

While we read John 9 through the eyes of the evangelist and his struggling church, we must take account of the fact that here, as in many places in the Gospels, later polemical issues, which were current at the time of the writing of these documents, were situated by the evangelists in the context of the life and ministry of Jesus.

The hostility in the Gospels towards the Pharisees, for example, is to be seen in this light. If we read these sacred texts more closely, we will discover that Jesus had much in common with the Pharisees.[1] The close affinities between their teaching and his, in content and in method, might explain the Pharisees' willingness to extend table fellowship to him (cf. Lk 7:36) — an invitation not lightly given.

Dramatic qualities

In keeping with the trial atmosphere which pervades the whole of the Fourth Gospel, the evangelist records the miracle and the confrontations it occasions in a sequence of seven interrogations. Though this dialogue in conflict situations would be enough to ensure the dramatic quality of the narrative, we could list among other contributing factors: the gradual introduction of significant detail, the observance of the classical law of stage duality in the structuring of the scenes, the anonymity of all the characters apart from Jesus himself, and the saving of the punchline to the very end of the story.

We could also note the way in which John has skilfully tied the whole narrative together by the effective use of the device called inclusion*. He begins his story with the disciples' question on the relationship between sin and physical blindness (9:2); and he brings it to a close with Jesus' teaching on the link between sin and spiritual blindness (9:41).

These observations are of more than mere literary interest; for, as O'Day (1987:53-75) has ably demonstrated,

---

[1] In this connection, see Kelly (1983) and Lee (1988:96-118).

the narrative dynamics are themselves revelatory. The meaning of a text is to be sought not only in what is said but also in how it is said.

Literary/dramatic analysis

There are many ways in which the material in John 9 can be divided. Ellis (1984:158), for example, proposes a five figure chiasm* which highlights the Pharisees' rejection of the testimony of the man's parents who fear their possible expulsion from the synagogue.

More helpful for our purpose, however, is the following schema which follows the divisions suggested by Martyn (1979:24-36):

Scene		Participants
1.	9:1-7	Jesus, disciples, man born blind
2.	9:8-12	neighbours, man born blind
3.	9:13-17	Pharisees, man born blind
4.	9:18-23	Pharisees, parents of the man
5.	9:24-34	Pharisees, man born blind
6.	9:35-38	Jesus, man born blind
7.	9:39-41	Jesus, Pharisees

The reader may find it a useful exercise at this point to write down (or otherwise take note of) the various questions that are asked in these scenes, identifying the points at issue, the questioner(s) and the respondent(s), and what is at stake for those concerned. It should be clear that, even when Jesus is physically absent from the scene (as he is for most of the story), he is nonetheless the real subject of the interrogations (cf. O'Day 1987:56).

Anonymity and lack of detail

The anonymity of the characters, as was stated above without elaboration, may serve the writer's dramatic

Day Three

purpose. At the very least it highlights the role of Jesus himself who is at once the evangelist's focus, the healed man's benefactor and the Pharisees' target.

It also lends weight to the pastoral thrust of the narrative. The fact that the man born blind is not named makes it easier for us, who must acknowledge our own spiritual blindness, to identify with him in our need for the enlightenment which Jesus alone can give. We may see in this man a representative figure of all whose obedience to the word of the Lord empowers them to receive the inestimable gift of faith.

A close reader of the text will also note that we are not told when or where the encounter between Jesus and the afflicted man takes place, even though John is sometimes very precise in recording such details (4:6; 19:13-14). It may be in the vicinity of the Temple; for the man is a beggar (9:8; cf. Acts 3:1-3) who probably sets himself up each day in a place where people congregate. At any rate, it is within easy walking distance of the Pool of Siloam.

The writer does not explicitly state that the cure takes place during the Feast of Tabernacles* (see 7:2); but, given the position of the story in the Gospel and its references to light and water, it is thematically linked to that feast and must be interpreted accordingly.

These omissions in no way detract from the story. Indeed they underline its enduring and universal relevance. What was once very timely in the pastorate of the evangelist is timeless in its application to the spiritual lives of those who seek God.

Old Testament background

There is only one instance of a cure from physical blindness in the whole of the Hebrew Scriptures. It is to be found in the Book of Tobit in a story which is a happy blend of oriental folklore and Jewish piety. Tobit is healed of his malady through the intervention of the angel Raphael who has been sent to him by God (Tob 5:10; 11:7-13).

Even among the few prophets to whom miracles are attributed, of none is it said that he cured a person of blindness. As the Psalmist proclaims, this is a divine prerogative: 'The LORD gives sight to the blind' (Ps 146:8; cf. Ex 4:11).

It will also be a sign of the messianic era. 'On that day the deaf shall hear the words of a book; and out of gloom and darkness, the eyes of the blind shall see,' writes the prophet Isaiah (Is 29:18, cf. 35:5; 42:7).

Jesus includes the restoration of sight to the blind among his messianic credentials both when he preaches in the synagogue at Nazareth (Lk 4:16-21) and when he replies to the query put to him by the disciples of the Baptist, 'Are you the one who is to come, or should we look for another?' (Mt 11:2-6 // Lk 7:18-23).

Synoptic parallels

Strictly speaking, there are no exact parallels in the Synoptic Gospels to the miracle recorded in John 9. Nowhere in those Gospels is a cure performed in favour of a person who has been afflicted from birth. Moreover, the Synoptic writers have a different understanding of Jesus' miracles. Where John sees them as signs *(sēmeia)* whereby occurrences in the natural order point to even greater effects in the order of grace, they speak of them as acts of power *(dunameis)* by means of which Jesus inaugurates the Kingdom* of God (see especially Mt 12:22-28).

Day Three

However, Matthew, Mark and Luke do include stories in which Jesus restores sight to the blind. In every case it is a blind man or blind men who are involved.[2]

Pastoral concerns

Finally, to assist our appreciation of the deeper meaning of John's account of the cure of the man born blind, we might identify some of the pastoral concerns which prompted him to include it in his Gospel. The issues he addresses include: the pain experienced by members of his community as a result of their expulsion from the synagogues, the Jewish-Christian debate about the identity of Jesus, and the recidivist tendencies of some of his flock whose faith was weak.

Detailed commentary

Scene 1 (9:1-7)

[1]As he passed by he saw a man blind from birth. [2]His disciples asked him, 'Rabbi, who sinned, this man or his parents, that he was born blind?' [3]Jesus answered, 'Neither he nor his parents sinned; it is so that the works of God might be made visible through him. [4]We have to do the works of the one who sent me while it is day. Night is coming when no one can work. [5]While I am in the world, I am the light of the world.' [6] When he had said this, he spat on the ground and made clay with the saliva, and smeared the clay on his eyes, [7]and said to him, 'Go wash in the Pool of Siloam' (which means Sent). So he went and washed, and came back able to see.

---

[2] At some later date it might be useful to read these Synoptic stories with the help of a book of Gospel parallels which would highlight their similarities and their significant differences. See: Mk 8:22-26; Mt 20:29-34 // Mk 10:46-52 // Lk 18:35-43; and Mt 9:27-31.

At first glance, the observation with which the story begins might appear to do nothing more than set the scene for the encounter between Jesus and the man born blind. However, for the early Christians from a Jewish background, the technical phrase, 'passed by', was rich in its associations. It is used in the Hebrew Scriptures to signify a theophany (that is, a manifestation of the divine presence), as in this passage from the Book of Exodus:

> Then Moses said, 'Do let me see your glory!' He answered, 'I will make all my beauty pass before you, and in your presence I will pronounce my name, "LORD"; I who show favors to whom I will, I who grant mercy to whom I will. But my face you cannot see, for no man sees me and still lives.' 'Here,' continued the LORD, 'is a place where you shall station yourself on the rock. When my glory passes I will set you in the hollow of the rock and will cover you with my hand until I have passed by. Then I will remove my hand, so that you may see my back; but my face is not to be seen' (Ex 33:18-23; cf. 1 Kings 19:9-18).

The response that Jesus gives to his disciples' question lends weight to this inference: 'Neither he nor his parents sinned; it is *so that the works of God might be made visible* through him' (9:3).

We have already commented on the man's anonymity. In this connection Duke (1985:118), drawing our attention to the fact that the definite article is missing in the Greek original, makes an interesting observation: 'He is not even called *tis anthrōpos*, but simply *anthrōpos*, thus de-emphasising his particularity and hinting that for John all humankind is born blind. The disciples are present only as foils.'

What are we to make of the question, strange to our way of thinking, that they put to Jesus? If we take account of the theology of Jesus' day, it is not as unusual as it might first appear. Popular wisdom held that blindness from birth or similar misfortunes might be attributed to the personal sin (even prenatal! cf. Gen 25:22) of the one afflicted or, more commonly, to the sin of one's parents.[3]

Jesus, in replying to his disciples' question, denies that there is any connection between the unfortunate man's defect and the moral behaviour of anyone. This is not necessarily inconsistent with his admonition to the man whom he healed of lameness: 'Look, you are well; do not sin any more, so that nothing worse may happen to you' (5:14). If illness is not a punishment for sin, it is undeniably a not uncommon consequence of it.

What is important to Jesus is not the cause of the man's blindness but its purpose in God's scheme of things. As with the death of Lazarus (11:4), 'it is so that the works of God might be made visible through him' (9:3; cf. 3:21). The significance of the miracle is thus pointed out even before it is performed.

Using what was probably a proverbial saying, Jesus goes on to compare his saving mission with a day's work (cf. 5:17) which will come to an end with the night in which he is delivered up to death (13:30). There is a sense of urgency in what he has to say here and on other occasions (cf. 7:33-34; 8:21; 12:35-36; 13:33).

It is interesting to note that Jesus speaks here in the plural: **'We** have to do ....' There is a part to be played, therefore, by his followers, his co-workers (1 Cor 3:9), in

---

[3] Belief that the sins of parents could be visited on their children is clearly indicated in this passage from Exodus:
'For I, the LORD, your God, am a jealous God, inflicting punishment for their fathers' wickedness on the children of those who hate me, down to the third and fourth generation' (Ex 20:5).
However, it is immediately added by way of counterbalance that the God who punishes sin (cf. Ps 89:32-33) is even more prodigal in 'bestowing mercy down to the thousandth generation, on the children of those who love [him] and keep [his] commandments' (Ex 20:6).

accomplishing the work of God (cf. 6:29). He himself is 'the light of the world' (9:5; 8:12) which makes it possible for them to carry on his mission.

This being said, the disciples disappear from the scene, having no further part to play in the story.

What was the blind man thinking as he listened to this strange conversation? He has been largely ignored till now; and even at this point he does not speak. Unlike the blind beggar, Bartimaeus (Mk 10:47 // Mt 20:30 // Lk 18:38), he does not cry out beseechingly. As O'Day (1987:59) observes, 'The blind man voices neither his need nor his faith.'

Jesus himself takes the initiative as he so often does in the Fourth Gospel, asking nothing of the man but his obedience. Healing in this case will precede faith which will then be seen more clearly for what it truly is — pure gift.

No sooner has Jesus declared himself to be the 'light of the world' than he spits on the ground and makes a paste with which he anoints the man's eyes. It is important that Jesus, who will later invite the 'unseeing' Thomas to touch him (20:27), should make physical contact with the one person present who cannot see him. This abrupt transition from exalted discourse to very mundane action might jolt us into asking with Bligh (1966:134): 'Why did Christ use such crude means to perform such a splendid miracle?'[4]

In Jesus' activity of making clay and spreading it on the eyes of the man blind from birth, we may have an echo

---

[4] It is not sufficient to note that spittle miracles are recorded in Mark's Gospel (Mk 7:33 — a deaf mute; and 8:23 — a blind man) or that saliva was believed in some parts of the ancient world to have medicinal properties. John is more subtle than that.

Day Three

of what took place 'in the beginning' (cf. 1:1) in the creation of Adam (Gen 2:5-7).

Furthermore, and very germane to the writer's purpose, the scene is now set for a confrontation between Jesus and his opponents; for the making of a paste by kneading mud is a breach of the sabbath regulations.

The blind man obeys Jesus' command without question (contrast Naaman's response to Elisha in 2 Kings 5:9-12). Even though Jesus does not tell him explicitly that he will be cured, he goes and washes in the Pool of Siloam. This rather large pool was fed by water diverted westward from the spring of Gihon by means of a tunnel that King Hezekiah had caused to be constructed (see 2 Chron 32:30; 2 Kings 20:20; Sir 48:17).

The beggar returns able to see for the first time in his life. Unlike Thomas, who will refuse to accept the word of the disciples (20:25), he happily invests his trust in Jesus' own life-giving word. Indeed, as Gillick (1985:90) states:

> He had to trust, and if he was to receive his sight his trust had to move him physically. Receiving his sight depended on entrusting the mystery of his darkness to the healing promise of Jesus.

That we are not told anything about his reaction to the miraculous cure, is consistent with John's general lack of attention to psychological data (contrast Acts 3:8 and 14:10 — men crippled from birth). We can only surmise how he feels when he sees the dazzling illumination of the Temple area for the first time.

It is noteworthy that Jesus is not at all paternalistic in his approach to the man born blind. He does not merely 'say the word' to the helpless one as he does in healing the lame man (5:8); nor does he lead him to the pool. Jesus mixes the mud; it is up to the man himself to do the rest.

Siloam, the evangelist tells us, means 'Sent'. This is significant in a Gospel in which Jesus is referred to repeatedly as 'the one sent' (cf. 9:4). It is almost a soubriquet for the Saviour who is quite literally a 'God-send' for all humankind.

Read within the context of the Feast of Tabernacles (see Lev 23:33-43; Num 29:12-39; Deut 16:13-15), this event becomes more than just another miracle story. When we recall that the Temple courts were illuminated by night during the feast and that there was a solemn libation of water drawn from the Pool of Siloam (cf. 7:37-38), it is clearly a *sign* in the special sense that John attaches to that word. As Marsh (1968:379) notes: 'The blind man demonstrates that Jesus fulfils the feast as both the one who commands the life-giving water and he who shines as the light of the world.'

Scene 2 (9:8-12)

> [8] His neighbours and those who had seen him earlier as a beggar said, 'Isn't this the one who used to sit and beg?' [9] Some said, 'It is,' but others said, 'No, he just looks like him.' He said, 'I am.' [10] So they said to him, '[So] how were your eyes opened?' [11] He replied, 'The man called Jesus made clay and anointed my eyes and told me, "Go to Siloam and wash." So I went there and washed and was able to see.' [12] And they said to him, 'Where is he?' He said, 'I don't know.'

Like the son of the royal official (4:51) the blind beggar is healed not in Jesus' presence but at a distance. When he returns from Siloam, Jesus, whom he has yet to see in the flesh, has left the scene. He is confronted instead by his neighbours who pose three questions.

Perhaps he appreciates the irony of the first of these queries and his townspeople's disagreement as to whether he is the man who used to sit and beg. He intrudes to assert that he is indeed that man; but, in view of his cure, he might truly add that he is a 'new' man. Both of their answers are correct.

Day Three

Translated literally, the man's very first words in the story are 'I am', which is the divine name (Ex 3:14). This suggests, as Marsh (1968:380) rather nicely puts it, that: 'some contagion of divinity remains with the healed man'.

The interrogation continues. Apparently unable to share his joy, his questioners are concerned to find out how his sight was restored (cf. 9:15,19,26). Clearly, though he has been healed of his blindness, they have not yet been 'cured' of their ignorance. They are more preoccupied with acceptable means than with desirable ends.

It may well be that the writer's own community had been subjected to such repeated questioning, in which case they could empathise with the man born blind while endeavouring to follow his example.

More free than he has ever been before, he stands on his own feet. No one speaks on his behalf, not even Jesus. He who has been silent for so long now becomes almost garrulous.

In response to his neighbours' questioning, he identifies his benefactor as 'the man called Jesus'. As he moves by stages towards faith, we will notice a progression in the ways in which he refers to Jesus: 'man' (9:11), 'a prophet' (9:17), '[a man] from God' (9:33), 'Lord' (9:38). A similar progression may be observed in the coming to faith of the Samaritan woman (4:9,11,19,29,42).

An attentive reader of John's narrative will discern a subtle and dramatically effective counterpoint to the man's development. As his faith in Jesus increases, that of his interrogators decreases. This, as we will see, is especially true of some of the Pharisees.[5]

---

5   At the risk of being repetitious, may I emphasise that John's portrayal of Jesus' opponents is coloured by the tension that existed between his own community and the Pharisees in the latter part of the first century C.E. The Gospel writers'

The final question in this scene, 'Where is he?', is not the question of genuine seekers after truth (for example, Mary Magdalen in 20:2,13). These people look for evidence that will convict, not for knowledge that will enlighten. Their enquiry meets with a blunt negative response from the man who is becoming both more confident and more frustrated.

Scene 3 (9:13-17)

> [13] They brought the one who was once blind to the Pharisees. [14] Now Jesus had made clay and opened his eyes on a sabbath. [15] So then the Pharisees also asked him how he was able to see. He said to them, 'He put clay on my eyes, and I washed, and now I can see.' [16] So some of the Pharisees said, 'This man is not from God, because he does not keep the sabbath.' [But] others said, 'How can a sinful man do such signs?' And there was a division among them. [17] So they said to the blind man again, 'What do you have to say about him, since he opened your eyes?' He said, 'He is a prophet.'

As a dramatic device to change the scene, the evangelist now has the man's neighbours bring him to the Pharisees. At the time that the Johannine community was taking shape, these dedicated laymen were the dominant force in Jewish society. Needless to say, the man born blind would have been slow to approach them of his own volition.

Only at this point in the story do we learn that Jesus effected the cure on a sabbath day (cf. 5:9-10; 7:22-23). This was a provocative action because the sabbath law

---

negative appraisal of the Pharisees, which provoked anti-Semitism among some Christians of later generations, hardly does justice to the true character of these Jewish leaders or to their historical importance. With justifiable pride Paul speaks of himself as a Pharisee (cf. Phil 3:5; Acts 23:6; 26:5).

Day Three

forbade 39 specific activities, including works of healing and kneading.

Concerned about respect for their sacred traditions and about strict observance of the Law*, the Pharisees continue the interrogation and insist on knowing how the man recovered his sight. Rather more briefly this time, the man repeats the details he has given to his neighbours (cf. 9:11). Once again his response leads to division among his questioners (cf. 7:45-52). In Duke's (1985:120) words, 'A *schisma* ensues between those who have seen the sign and those who have seen the sinner.'

Some, at least, of the Pharisees stubbornly refuse to consider the miracle Jesus has performed. The clear evidence of the man's good fortune is less important to them than any evidence they can marshall against Jesus. For them there is no progession of titles accorded to Jesus whom they repeatedly refer to simply as 'this man' (9:16,24,29).

Their blind spot prevents them from seeing that Jesus has indeed come forth from God — a claim he himself frequently makes (see, among other texts, 8:42).

There is a certain irony in the Pharisees' parting question. This time they want to know not merely the facts of the case but what the man thinks of Jesus. Previously they would hardly have asked a blind beggar's opinion on any matter of consequence such as this.

The best answer he can come up with is, 'He is a prophet' (cf. 4:19 — the Samaritan woman; Mt 16:14 and parallels; Mt 21:11,46). This observation may point to some growth in the man's faith; but he still has a long way to go before he bows in Jesus' presence in an attitude of worship (9:38).

In passing, we may note that the only prophets to whom miracles are attributed are Moses, Elijah and Elisha.

Scene 4 (9:18-23)

¹⁸Now the Jews did not believe that he had been blind and gained his sight until they summoned the parents of the one who had gained his sight. ¹⁹They asked them, 'Is this your son, who you say was born blind? How does he now see?' ²⁰His parents answered and said, 'We know that this is our son and that he was born blind. ²¹We do not know how he sees now, nor do we know who opened his eyes. Ask him, he is of age; he can speak for himself.' ²²His parents said this because they were afraid of the Jews, for the Jews had already agreed that if anyone acknowledged him as the Messiah, he would be expelled from the synagogue. ²³For this reason his parents said, 'He is of age; question him.'

For pastoral and apologetic* reasons John contrasts in his Gospel the perverse unbelief of those who reject Jesus (see 1:11) and the testimony of those who, like the man born blind and members of his own community, bear witness to him. His shorthand expression for those who oppose Jesus is 'the Jews'.[6]

The parents of the man are summoned and interrogated. Among the three questions put to them by 'the Jews', the question of how he gained his sight is posed for the third time.

The parents seem to be aware of the authorities' hidden agenda; for, having given predictable answers to the first two questions, they claim to know neither how their son was cured nor by whom. They suggest that, since he is old enough to give valid testimony, he himself should be approached.

---

[6] All told, and by no means always with negative overtones, John uses the term 'the Jews' 71 times (cf. Mt 5x, Mk 5x, Lk 5x). It should not be construed as anti-Semitic in any of its contexts. John, himself a Jew, readily acknowledges the Jewishness of Jesus (cf. 18:35) who affirms, in his conversation with the Samaritan woman, that 'salvation is from the Jews' (4:22).

Day Three 145

The reason given for their reticence (it is surely a later editorial addition) is thought by most commentators to be an anachronistic allusion to the trauma of many of the early Christians who, by the time the Fourth Gospel was written, had been expelled from the synagogues (see 12:42; 16:2; Mt 10:17 // Mk 13:9 // Lk 21:12). This formal excommunication of those who proclaimed Jesus as the Messiah (cf. Acts 2:31,36) began about 90 C.E. after the Council of Jamnia. Doubtless it caused some painful divisions within families (cf. Mt 10:34-36 // Lk 12:51-53).

We could point to other examples in the Fourth Gospel of people who fear to act because of 'the Jews' (7:13; 19:38; 20:19). The man born blind, however, is not among them; and for this reason he is proposed to the members of the evangelist's community as a model of the true disciple, resolutely standing his ground in the face of conflict. Perhaps it may be said of him, in the writer's own words, that true love has cast out fear (1 Jn 4:18).

Scene 5 (9:24-34)

[24]So a second time they called the man who had been blind and said to him, 'Give God the praise! We know that this man is a sinner.' [25]He replied, 'If he is a sinner, I do not know. One thing I do know is that I was blind and now I see.' [26]So they said to him, 'What did he do to you? How did he open your eyes?' [27]He answered them, 'I told you already and you did not listen. Why do you want to hear it again? Do you want to become his disciples, too?' [28]They ridiculed him and said, 'You are that man's disciple; we are disciples of Moses! [29]We know that God spoke to Moses, but we do not know where this one is from.' [30]The man answered and said to them, 'This is what is so amazing, that you do not know where he is from, yet he opened my eyes. [31]We know that God does not listen to sinners, but if one is devout and does his will, he listens to him. [32]It is unheard of that anyone ever opened the eyes of a person

born blind. ³³If this man were not from God, he would not be able to do anything.' ³⁴They answered and said to him, 'You were born totally in sin, and are you trying to teach us?' Then they threw him out.

'The Jews' (probably some of the Pharisees, as in Martyn's schema above) now subject the man born blind to a second round of questions. They begin rather more aggressively than before by placing him under an oath to tell the truth, 'Give God the praise!' (cf. Josh 7:19). The situation is doubly ironic because that is precisely what the man is doing by witnessing to Jesus and what his questioners are not doing by refusing to acknowledge the hand of God in the sign that Jesus has wrought. It is they, who gratuitously call Jesus a sinner, who are the real sinners (9:41; cf. 8:46). Duke (1985:121) comments incisively:

> 'The Jews' invoke the name of God to deny the work of God; they command the man to speak the truth, and in the next breath they prove they are closed to the truth; emphatically they shout what they *know* and prove their utter ignorance.

At this point in the story only the man born blind stands up for Jesus. More interested in the facts of his miraculous cure than in fruitless debating, he openly admits both what he knows and what he does not know. With good reason we may see him, in whom acerbic wit and honest judgment find voluble expression when occasion requires it, as the apologist of the Johannine community in its polemic against the disciples of Moses towards the end of the first century (cf. Heb 3:1-6; Jn 1:17).

Yet again these tediously repetitive and very persistent men of 'means' ask him: 'What did he do to you? How did he open your eyes?' In exasperation the man rebukes them and, touching them where they are most vulnerable, he calls on them in effect to declare their hand. By asking them if they *too* are thinking of becoming Jesus' disciples, he may be implying that he himself has already made

Day Three

that step. His question is reminiscent of one that the Pharisees addressed to Nicodemus in an earlier confrontation (7:52).

The authorities, unconscious yet again of the irony of their utterance, resort to ridicule. If they are in fact worthy disciples of Moses, as they claim to be, they should recognise Jesus for who he truly is. As Jesus said to his unresponsive hearers on the previous occasion that he healed on a sabbath day:

> 'Do not think that I will accuse you before the Father: the one who will accuse you is Moses, in whom you have placed your hope. For if you had believed Moses, you would have believed me, because he wrote about me. But if you do not believe his writings, how will you believe my words?' (5:45-47).

For the first time, speaking rather disparagingly of him as 'this one' (as in 9:16,24), the Pharisees admit their ignorance of Jesus' origins. Both here and on a previous occasion (7:27), when 'the Jews' did claim to know where Jesus was from, the subtle irony of the fourth evangelist is at work. Had he been present during this interrogation, Jesus might have repeated his statement: '... I know where I came from and where I am going. But you do not know where I come from or where I am going' (8:14).

The man born blind is in control of the situation as he continues to witness to Jesus; the one who is accounted foolish is confounding the wise (cf. 1 Cor 1:27). Using their own terms and perhaps mischievously echoing their 'we know' (9:29), he takes his questioners to task. For him, Jesus must be a man of God because 'God does not listen to sinners' (cf. Prov 15:29; Is 1:15).

He reminds them that no one (not even Moses, we might add) has ever before opened the eyes of a man born blind. His logic is good; but their hearts are unmoved. Well does Jesus say later, during his supper discourse: 'If I had not done works among them that no one else ever did, they would not have sin; but as it is, they have seen and hated both me and my Father' (15:24).

Coming closer to making an act of faith in Jesus worthy of a disciple, the man born blind acknowledges that Jesus must surely come from God. 'If this man were not from God,' he reasons, 'he would not be able to do anything' (cf. 9:16).

In their retort, 'You were totally born in sin, and are you trying to teach us?', the Pharisees implicitly admit that the man had been blind from birth (cf. 9:2). Note the irony of this rhetorical question. The roles are reversed; for the beggar man has truly become the authentic teacher.

There is a rather terrible finality about the blunt observation which concludes the scene, 'Then they threw him out.' But the end is not yet in sight.

Scene 6 (9:35-38)

> 35When Jesus heard that they had thrown him out, he found him and said, 'Do you believe in the Son of Man?' 36He answered and said, 'Who is he, sir, that I may believe in him?' 37Jesus said to him, 'You have seen him and the one speaking with you is he.' 38He said, 'I do believe, Lord,' and he worshiped him.

Jesus, who has been notably absent from the scene, returns. Good shepherd that he is (10:1-18), he takes the initiative in seeking the man out and asks him if he believes in the Son of Man — surely the most crucial of all the questions addressed to the man who had spent so many years in darkness. It is asked lovingly by one whose purpose is not to extract evidence but to impart wisdom. This is the man's *kairos** moment, his opportunity to do in faith what was asked of him before rather contemptuously, 'Give God the praise!' (9:24).

Day Three

The title 'Son of Man', which Jesus uses on this occasion, is his own preferred way of referring to himself. It has overtones of judgment (as in Dan 7:13-15) which prepare us for the confrontation with the Pharisees in the final scene.

What is going through the mind of the formerly blind man who has waited until now to see his benefactor? Doubtless, after his ordeal, he finds Jesus' demeanour reassuring; and, open to the mystery of this man who speaks with authority, he asks him, 'Who is he, sir, that I may believe in him?'

In words reminiscent of his self-disclosure to the Samaritan woman (4:26), Jesus replies, 'You have seen him and the one speaking with you is he.'

We have reached the climactic moment in the faith journey of the man who had been blind from birth. He has received from Jesus the gift of physical sight — an outward sign of the 'light of life' (8:12), that even more wonderful gift of insight which enables him to confess, in the words of an early baptismal creed, 'I do believe, Lord.' Now truly one of the 'children of the light' (12:36) in the fullest sense, he worships Jesus (cf. Mt 28:9).

The Pharisees who interrogated him, on the other hand, though blessed with the physical gift of vision from birth, remain blind to the spiritual realities which Jesus reveals in word and work (cf. 3:19-21).

Apropos to these matters, McPolin (1976:415) quotes Helen Keller:
> I have walked with people whose eyes are full of light but who see nothing in sea or sky, nothing in city streets, nothing in books. It were far better to sail forever in the night of blindness ... than to be content with the mere act of seeing. The only lightless dark is the night of darkness in ignorance and insensibility.

Scene 7 (9:39-41)

³⁹Then Jesus said, 'I came into this world for judgment, so that those who do not see might see, and those who do see might become blind.' ⁴⁰Some of the Pharisees who were with him heard this and said to him, 'Surely we are not also blind, are we?' ⁴¹Jesus said to them, 'If you were blind, you would have no sin; but now you are saying, "We see," so your sin remains.'

According to O'Day (1987:73): 'Verse 39 is the hermeneutical* key to interpreting the entire chapter.' Like Pilate (18:38), some of the Pharisees, as portrayed by John, cannot see Truth when it stands before them in the person of Jesus. Interestingly enough, as the spotlight falls on them, the word 'judgment' is used for the first time in the chapter. It is the more dramatically effective for being so cleverly withheld.

The judgment has already been pronounced in Jesus' discourse to Nicodemus: 'And this is the verdict, that the light came into the world, but people preferred darkness to light, because their works were evil' (3:19; cf. 15:22-24). The light which reveals is also the light which exposes.

What a consummate ironist John is in having the Pharisees address their final question to Jesus — the real target of all their enquiries — in these terms, 'Surely we are not also blind, are we?'

In responding to them Jesus drives home the point that their spiritual blindness is a form of culpable ignorance. Whereas the man they persecuted was born blind, they will die blind to the light of God's Son (cf. Mt 23:16-17). Sin and blindness (cf. 9:2) are related after all — dramatically, a nice concluding touch.

2. IMAGINATIVE PRAYER WITH THE MAN BORN BLIND

Begin by joining the man born blind in his home prior to his departure for the Temple precincts where he spends his days seeking alms from passers-by. Take in the world of material poverty and sensory deprivation that is his. Then walk slowly with him as, begging bowl in hand, he treads a familar path to his chosen site.

As you enter into his persona, you become more conscious than heretofore of the sounds that assail your ears — the crunch of sandalled feet on paving stones, the babble of anonymous voices, the clamour of merchants selling their wares, the clatter of an occasional coin in your cup.

At one point, you become the unwilling focus of attention of an itinerant rabbi and his disciples who have stopped nearby, discussing the origins of your blindness. One of them asks whether your condition is due to your sinfulness or that of your parents. How do you feel about this unfeeling intrusion into your private space?

Listen as Jesus responds to their enquiry (have you heard his voice before?). Feel his gentle touch as he spreads a muddy paste on your sightless eyes. He speaks to you lovingly as one who has authority and you are constrained to carry out his command to go and wash at Siloam.

What are your thoughts as you make your way there accompanied by helpers and curious hangers-on? Experience the coolness of the water as you bathe your face. Its reflected image is the first thing you see in your entire lifetime. What is your emotional response to the new world that opens before you (joy, confusion, gratitude, disbelief, fear, ...)? How do the bystanders react?

Endure the interrogations of the tediously incredulous people who persist in asking you how the supposed miracle took place. New resources of self-assurance, courage, and even wit are now available to you as you parry the thrusts of the Pharisees who treat you with more disdain than you ever experienced as a beggar. What are your feelings as they bring this heated interchange to a conclusion by casting you out?

In the midst of your confusion you are once more terribly alone, rejected by people (some, at least, of whom appear to be complacently self-righteous) and an embarrassment to your parents. A man approaches; you hear a familiar voice and, for the first time, you see the face of the 'prophet' who has turned your life upside down. His question to you is a compellingly liberating invitation to become his disciple. 'I do believe, Lord,' you say; and you fall at his feet.

Stay with your feelings at this point, extending your dialogue with Jesus as the Spirit moves you.

3. PRAYING WITH JESUS

Having identified with the man born blind in his journey to faith and having felt with him the impact of Jesus' words and deeds, endeavour in this session to plumb more deeply the mystery of our Saviour's love by joining him in his prayer to the God whom he addresses as 'Abba'.

To enter imaginatively into that prayer, review the touching story of the cure of the beggarman from the perspective of Jesus. What does Jesus bring to his intimate conversation with his heavenly Father from the events of this day?

His compassionate heart, moved at first by the sorry plight of the blind man, was more deeply touched by his unquestioning obedience and his eventual confession of faith. How refreshingly different, in retrospect, the generous openness of this social outcast appears to him compared with the increasing hostility of so many of the people who reject his teaching and who, at a profound level, are blind even to their blindness.

What hopes does Jesus entertain for this new disciple who has witnessed to him in the face of opposition similar to that which he himself has experienced?

4. CONTEXTUAL PRAYER

Faith/discipleship/witness. Adult converts to Christianity make a journey from faith to baptism whereas 'cradle' Christians (at least, in the mainline churches) face a journey from baptism to faith. The task of the latter is to appropriate personally, at some point in time, the confession of faith which their sponsors made on their behalf when they were sacramentally admitted to the community of believers.

As we reflect upon the faith journey of the man born blind (with its baptismal overtones), we might ask ourselves such questions as these: Have I settled for a fellow-traveller's religion (largely human in origin) or have I embraced a disciple's faith (wholly God-given)? Have I said and do I repeat with conviction my own 'I do believe, Lord'? Does my faith express itself, when occasion demands, in courageous witness or am I, like the beggar's parents, timid and afraid?

Spiritual blindness. To a greater or lesser degree, we are all afflicted with a form of blindness. It is a universal malady which finds expression in irrational prejudices, imperceptive judgments, and insensitivity to the plight of others. Our unwillingness to admit to this condition may be one of the clearest symptoms of the disease.

To be blind to our blindness is to remain in need of healing, condemned rather than cured. The light cannot penetrate our darkness until we trustingly tread the path to Siloam ourselves, conscious of the fact that the Lord's command to wash is addressed to all without exception.

It could be that we are at best partially sighted with respect to what Gillick (1985:88) calls 'the deeper realities, the divine "coincidence" of the constantly "eye-opening" love of God in all the events of our lives.' Worse still, lacking sometimes in good works, we may have reason to identify with those who will be forced to admit on judgment day that they could not see Christ in their suffering sisters and brothers (cf. Mt 25:41-46).

We might pray for the enlightenment always to see God through the eyes of Christ and to see all created reality (especially ourselves and our less than perfect neighbours) through the eyes of our compassionate God. Hopefully, while acknowledging our sinfulness, we will not be blind to our many good qualities. A poor self-image is often the result of defective vision.

Of course, there will always be limits to what we can see in this life which derive not from any ill-will on our part but from the limitations of a human condition wherein people of faith look forward with hope to 'what eye has not seen' (1 Cor 2:9). A mature spiritual life in these circumstances, to quote Gillick (1985:88) again, can be nothing other than 'the living honestly within the confines of not seeing clearly'.

Liberation. As we saw in yesterday's reflection on the story of the Samaritan woman, any encounter with Jesus is always a liberating experience for the person who is open to his revelation.

Jesus liberates the man born blind not only from the scourge of physical blindness but also from the degradation of enforced poverty and (from the perspective of the evangelist) from the shackles of a legalistic religion with its characteristic claims to superior knowledge.

5. PRAYING THE MANTRA

Among other possibilities, you might like to consider the following pertinent texts for use as a mantra:

Day Three

The LORD is my light and my salvation (Ps 27:1).
'I do believe, Lord' (Jn 9:38).
'Lord, please let me see' (Lk 18:41).
'In your light we see light' (Ps 36:10).

DAY FOUR

JESUS AND THE FAMILY AT BETHANY
(John 11:1-44; 12:1-11,17)

> The sages have a hundred maps to give
> That trace their scrawling cosmos like a tree,
> They rattle reason out through many a sieve
> That stores the sand and lets the gold go free:
> And all these things are less than dust to me
> Because my name is Lazarus and I live.
> (G.K. Chesterton, 'The Convert')

1. REFLECTIVE STUDY OF THE TEXT

Introduction

The prologue of John's Gospel has been likened to a musical overture in which key themes are announced. Pursuing this simile a little further, we might say that the whole Gospel is composed of variations on one of these themes — the theme of life. It is introduced in the opening bars; and it is part of the finale:

> What came to be through him was life, and this life was the light of the human race (1:4).

> But these [signs] are written that you may [come to] believe that Jesus is the Messiah, the Son of God, and that through this belief you may have life in his name. (20:31).

Jesus defines his mission in terms of the gift of life (10:10) — indeed, of 'eternal life' (10:28). To bring this mission to its fulfilment, when his hour has finally come, he stretches out his arms on the cross. In thus giving up his own life so that we might 'have life ... more abundantly', our Saviour not only reveals a love greater than we can comprehend (cf. 15:13) but also manifests the loving initiative of the Father whose envoy he is: 'In this way the love of God was revealed to us: God sent his only Son into the world so that we might have life through him' (1 Jn 4:9; cf. Jn 3:16).

This inestimable gift of eternal life, as Jesus assures his disciples, is the present possession of those who respond in faith to the words of 'spirit and life' (6:63) which he utters. 'Amen, amen, I say to you, whoever hears my word and believes in the one who sent me has eternal life ...' (5:24).

With these pertinent thoughts in mind, read aloud and with reverent attention the two readings allocated for the fourth day of our retreat; but, as on other days, let us first pause for a while and pray for the grace to know 'the only true God, and the one whom [he] sent, Jesus Christ' (17:3; cf. 1 Jn 5:20); for in this knowledge lies eternal life.

Identifying with Lazarus, you may like to conclude this introductory prayer with Psalm 129, the *De profundis*.

Preliminary observations
Foreshadowing the passion of Jesus

In our reflective study period today we will consider two events which take place at Bethany, involving the members of a family dear to the heart of Jesus — Martha, Mary and Lazarus (El-azar = 'God helps'). Both events, the raising of Lazarus and the anointing of Jesus' feet, are linked thematically and theologically with the writer's account of the passion and death of Jesus.

Going a step further, Schneiders (1987b:45) demonstrates how they form part of a sequence which proleptically* expresses the paschal* mystery:

11:47-53 Jesus is symbolically executed in the session of the Sanhedrin*;
12:1-8   Jesus is symbolically buried in the anointing scene;
12:17-18 Jesus is symbolically glorified in the triumphal entry into Jerusalem.

John, unlike the other three evangelists, makes the raising of Lazarus the proximate cause of Jesus' arrest (11:45-47). For the authorities, who had previously sought to apprehend and even to cause bodily injury to Jesus (7:32; 8:40,59; 10:31,39), it is the last straw.

For the Christian believer, on the other hand, this extraordinary sign (to use John's preferred word for Jesus' miracles) is clearly intended to foreshadow the events surrounding Jesus' own triumph over death. As almost all commentators point out, the evangelist draws a close parallel between the stories of the restoration of life to Lazarus and the resurrection of Jesus. Flanagan (1983:56) summarises it this way:

Both accounts speak of:

a mourning Mary at the tomb (11:31 and 20:11);
a cave tomb closed with a stone (11:38,41 and 20:1);
grave clothes plus a face cloth (11:44 and 20:67);
a special role given to Thomas (11:16 and 20:24-28).

With this in mind, we would do well to stress the symbolic and the theological in our reading of John 11 rather than the historical.

John and the Synoptic Gospels

John is not alone in relating a story in which Jesus restores life to a dead person. All three of the Synoptic

Gospels include the beautiful story of Jesus' intervention on behalf of the daughter of Jairus (Mt 9:18-19,23-26 // Mk 5:21-24,35-43 // Lk 8:40-42,49-56); and Luke relates the raising to life of the only son of the distraught widow of Nain (Lk 7:11-17). Moreover, in Matthew and Luke, Jesus includes the raising of the dead among his own 'credentials' (Mt 11:5 // Lk 7:22) — a notable addition to Is 35:5-6 and 61:1; and, in Matthew, he commands the Twelve not only to cure the sick but also to raise the dead to life (Mt 10:8).

However, John's account of the raising of Lazarus, in which Jesus intervenes on behalf of one of his own disciples, is undeniably the most striking miracle of its kind in the entire Bible; for Lazarus has been dead and buried for four days.

Another comparison which merits some attention concerns the Lazarus pericope* in John and the Lucan parable of the rich man and the poor beggar (Lk 16:19-31). Both stories tell of a man called Lazarus who dies; but we should not hasten to draw conclusions from that fact.

It may be purely coincidental that Luke's Lazarus is the only character mentioned by name in any of the New Testament parables and that his namesake in John is the only character (if we exclude the son of Timaeus in Mk 10:46) named in a miracle story.

It could be that Luke's parable is based on an historical event and that John has incorporated in his narrative of the raising of Lazarus some elements of this tradition.

Representative figures

Lazarus, who speaks not a word in the whole Gospel, is attentive to the voice of Jesus. When the Lord calls him from death to life, he obeys; and many others come to believe because of him (11:45; 12:11). For Culpepper

(1983:141) 'Lazarus, therefore, represents the disciple to whom life has been given and challenges the reader to accept the realisation of eschatological* expectations in Jesus.'

From John's depiction of Martha, we may see her as representative of those believers who, before the Parousia*, confess their faith in the final resurrection after death because they acknowledge Jesus to be the source of eternal life. Unlike Thomas, who must first see a sign if he is to believe (20:25), she proclaims Jesus to be the Christ even before he intervenes to restore her brother to her (11:27).

Mary does not appear to be blessed with the same insight as her sister. She does not verbalise her faith; but, in the extravagance of her love for Jesus, she nonetheless gives a splendid example of how a true disciple might be expected to act (12:3).

A nice distinction is made by E. Schüssler Fiorenza (1983:330) when she writes: 'While Martha of Bethany is responsible for the primary articulation of the community's Christological* faith, Mary of Bethany articulates the right praxis of discipleship.'

Detailed commentary

1. The Raising of Lazarus (11:1-44)

Setting the scene (11:1-6)

> [1]Now a man was ill, Lazarus from Bethany, the village of Mary and her sister Martha. [2]Mary was the one who had anointed the Lord with perfumed oil and dried his feet with her hair; it was her brother Lazarus who was ill. [3]So the sisters sent word to him, saying, 'Master, the one you love is ill.' [4]When Jesus heard this he said, 'This illness is not to end in death, but is for the glory of God, that the Son of God may be glorified through it.' [5]Now

Jesus loved Martha and her sister and Lazarus. ⁶So when he heard that he was ill, he remained for two days in the place where he was.

The scene is set for Jesus' seventh miracle by the very direct opening words of the chapter: 'Now a man was ill.' He is identified as Lazarus from Bethany — a small village, mentioned by all four evangelists (Mk 11:1 // Lk 19:28-29; Mt 26:6 // Mk 14:3), lying about three kilometres east of Jerusalem (11:18). He is the brother of Martha and Mary.

We are told by the writer, or more probably by the editor of the Gospel, that the Mary in question is 'the one who had anointed the Lord with perfumed oil and dried his feet with her hair.' This is an interesting piece of cross-referencing (a feature of the Fourth Gospel) inasmuch as the record of the event referred to is yet to come (12:1-3).

Like Mary of Nazareth at Cana (2:3), where Jesus first revealed his glory (2:11), they appeal confidently to him for help by merely stating a fact: 'Master, the one you love is ill.'

That the glory of God will once again be manifest through him is foreshadowed in his response to their plea: 'This illness is not to end in death, but is for the glory of God, that the Son of God may be glorified through it.' The event is interpreted even before it happens (cf. 9:3). There is a beautiful irony in this statement because, as the reader well knows, Lazarus' sickness does end in death — Jesus' own (cf. 11:53).

As in the Cana miracle (2:11), glory and faith are closely linked in this narrative of the raising of Lazarus (11:4, 14-15,25,26,27,40,42,45). This sign, like all the others in the Gospel, has been 'written that you may [come to] believe that Jesus is the Messiah, the Son of God, and that through this belief you may have life in his name' (20:31).

Day Four

Before concluding these introductory verses, the evangelist reminds us of the love that Jesus has for Lazarus (11:3; cf. 11:36) and his two sisters. The Gospel has both its beloved disciple and its beloved family.

Taking account of this intimate relationship, it may appear strange that Jesus chooses to remain with his disciples for two days at the other Bethany across the Jordan where John first baptised (1:28; cf. 10:40). He will, however, always do things in his own way and in his own good time. Recall his words to his brothers about travelling in Judea for the Feast of Tabernacles*: 'My time is not yet here, but the time is always right for you. ... You go up to the feast. I am not going up to this feast, because my time has not yet been fulfilled' (7:6,8). He does go up secretly to the feast a little later (7:10).[1]

Jesus' delay is interpreted by some commentators in the light of the early Church's concern at the delay of the Parousia*. The pastoral leader of the Johannine church, in this approach, included the story of the raising of Lazarus to allay the fears of some members of his community who were concerned about the fate of those who had died before the Lord's return (cf. 1 Thess 4:13-18; Rev 6:10; 14:13).

One writer who questions this point of view is Sandra Schneiders. She sees the primary issue as Jesus' mission to give life to all believers (cf. 10:10). The problem is then not death before the last day but death at all. For her (1987b:48):

> The theological concern of the Lazarus story, therefore, is not the delay of the parousia but the real meaning of

---

[1] Giblin (1980) has written an interesting study of a number of episodes in the Gospel in which Jesus proceeds to act positively after initially responding negatively to a suggestion. In addition to the above examples, consider: 2:4,8 — Cana; and 4:48,50 — the cure of the royal official's son.

death and life, of the absence and presence of Jesus. It is the problem of death in the community of eternal life.

First dialogue: Jesus and his disciples (11:7-16)[2]

[7]Then after this he said to his disciples, 'Let us go back to Judea.' [8]The disciples said to him, 'Rabbi, the Jews were just trying to stone you, and you want to go back there?' [9]Jesus answered, 'Are there not twelve hours in a day? If one walks during the day, he does not stumble, because he sees the light of this world. [10]But if one walks at night, he stumbles because the light is not in him.' [11]He said this, and then told them, 'Our friend Lazarus is asleep, but I am going to awaken him.' [12]So the disciples said to him, 'Master, if he is asleep, he will be saved.' [13]But Jesus was talking about his death, while they thought that he meant ordinary sleep. [14]So then Jesus said to them clearly, 'Lazarus has died. [15]And I am glad for you that I was not there, that you may believe. Let us go to him.' [16]So Thomas, called Didymus, said to his fellow disciples, 'Let us also go to die with him.'

After two days have passed, Jesus' suggestion that they should go back to Judea is not greeted with enthusiasm by his disciples. They point out that he has just had a narrow escape from stoning (10:31) while at the Feast of the Dedication* in Jerusalem.

His reply to their objection is couched in highly figurative language which is probably lost on them. There are in fact twelve hours in a Jewish working day (cf. Mt 20:1-16 — the parable of the labourers in the vineyard); but what Jesus is implying is that he must use to good effect the short time that remains to him before his death (cf. 9:4-5; 12:35-36).

He is aware that fidelity to his life-giving mission will continue to entail serious risks; but, good shepherd that

---

2 The division of the material into seven dialogues is based on Crossan (1967:101).

he is, he is prepared to lay down his life for his sheep (10:11; cf. 15:13). 'Our friend Lazarus is asleep,' he says, 'but I am going to awaken him' (cf. Mt 9:24 // Mk 5:39 // Lk 8:52 — Jairus's daughter).

Not surprisingly, the disciples fail to comprehend what he says because they persist in taking his words literally. Perhaps they are still intent, for their own sake, on dissuading him from making the journey to Jerusalem.

The truth of the matter is clarified when Jesus adds quite bluntly and with dramatic effect, 'Lazarus has died.' Where they lack understanding, the Johannine Jesus is possessed of superior knowledge (see, among many other texts, 1:48 and 4:16-18).

Though the death of his friend Lazarus will later move him to the very depths of being, Jesus indicates at this juncture that he is glad (for his disciples' sake) that he was not present at his passing. Knowing that their faith stands to benefit by what he will do (cf. 11:42), he invites them to travel to Bethany with him.

Thomas, the realist, speaks for the others when he acknowledges the dangerous nature of this mission. 'Let us also go and die with him,' he says. In view of the concern already expressed about Jesus' safety (11:8), it seems clear that the phrase 'with him' refers not to Lazarus, whom the chief priests will plot to kill after he has become something of a celebrity (12:9-11), but to Jesus himself.

Second dialogue: Jesus and Martha (11:17-27)

[17] When Jesus arrived, he found that Lazarus had already been in the tomb for four days. [18] Now Bethany was near Jerusalem, only about two miles away. [19] And many of the Jews had come to Martha and Mary to comfort them about their brother. [20] When Martha heard that Jesus was coming, she went to meet him; but Mary sat at home. [21] Martha said to Jesus, 'Lord, if you had

been here, my brother would not have died. [22][But] even now I know that whatever you ask of God, God will give you.' [23]Jesus said to her, 'Your brother will rise.' [24]Martha said to him, 'I know he will rise, in the resurrection on the last day.' [25]Jesus told her, 'I am the resurrection and the life; whoever believes in me, even if he dies, will live, [26]and everyone who lives and believes in me will never die. Do you believe this?' [27]She said to him, 'Yes, Lord. I have come to believe that you are the Messiah, the Son of God, the one who is coming into the world.'

As if anticipating the objections of sceptics, John reminds us several times that Lazarus is dead; indeed, he has been entombed for four days (11:14,17,39).[3]

Jewish tradition held that the spirit left the tomb area on the fourth day, which makes the raising of Lazarus even more remarkable than the 'resurrection' miracles recorded in the Synoptic Gospels, the Hebrew Scriptures (1 Kings 17:17-24; 2 Kings 13:21), or the Acts of the Apostles (Acts 9:36-42).

To this point the inactivity of Jesus has served the dramatic purpose of maintaining the tension. It now gives way to much rapid movement in keeping with heightened emotions. In this connection, Flanagan (1983:54) observes:

> The message of distress goes from Bethany near Jerusalem (v. 18) to Jesus .... Jesus and his disciples move toward Bethany. Martha and Mary move to Jesus. All move to the tomb. Lazarus moves out of the tomb. Informers move to the Pharisees. Jesus and his company move to Ephraim in northern Judea. *[Emphasis omitted]*.

---

3 It is quite possible that the evangelist is reacting here to gnostic* tendencies to which his community was exposed.

For much of the story the focus is on Martha and Mary rather than on their brother who does not utter a single word in the entire narrative.

Possibly wishing to speak to Jesus privately, it is Martha who responds first to the news that Jesus is approaching by going out to meet him. For her part, in keeping with the oriental custom of sitting and mourning at home, Mary is content to await his arrival. Their characters, thus revealed, are in keeping with the Lucan portrayal of them (Lk 10:38-42).

Martha greets Jesus with a statement of fact: 'Lord, if you had been here, my brother would not have died' — words which, in her turn, her sister Mary will repeat (11:32). Then, knowing that Jesus' prayers will not fail (cf. 9:31), she gives voice to the hope implicit in her statement by adding, '[But] even now I know that whatever you ask of God, God will give you.' She speaks with the confidence Jesus will later seek to instil in his disciples when he says to them at the last supper, 'If you ask anything of me in my name, I will do it.'

Jesus reassures Martha (and, we might add, reassures the Johannine community as well) by saying, 'Your brother will rise.' Not surprisingly, she thinks he is referring to the general resurrection of the dead; so she replies, 'I know he will rise on the last day.' Her eschatology is clearly *futurist*, whereas that of Jesus in 11:25 is *realised*. For him, eternal life is a present reality in the life of the believer (5:24; 1 Jn 5:11-13); and it will endure even should physical death (as indeed it must) intervene.

Jesus says to Martha, 'I am the resurrection and the life; whoever believes in me, even if he dies, will live, and everyone who lives and believes in me will never die' (11:25-26; cf. 4:14). His remark is profoundly self-revelatory; and it calls, therefore, for a response in faith. This is why he adds, 'Do you believe this?'

Theologically, this is the heart of the matter. Jesus Christ is truly the resurrection and the life for all who can say with Martha, 'Yes, Lord. I have come to believe that you are the Messiah, the Son of God, the one who is coming into the world' (11:27; cf. 20:31). He is the 'I am' who can give life both to those who have died and to those who mourn their passing (cf. Is 51:12; Mt 5:4). As we read in Paul's first letter to the Thessalonians: 'Our Lord Jesus Christ ... died for us, so that *whether we are awake or asleep* we may live together with him' (1 Thess 5:9-10).

Moule (1975:120) puts it well when he states: 'The believer, as both the Gospel and the First Epistle of St John say, has, because of his faith or his love, already passed from death to life, whatever his physical condition (John 5:24; 1 John 3:14).'

Just as the physical sight which the blind man receives at the hands of Jesus is a sign of the spiritual insight or faith with which he is gifted, so also is the restoration of earthly life to Lazarus a sign of the eternal life with which Jesus gifts believers both before and after their death.[4]

Martha's reply to Jesus' question is one of a series of public confessions in the Gospel (1:29,36; 1:49; 4:42; 6:68-69; 9:38; 12:13; 20:28,31). Using words attributed to Peter in the Synoptic Gospels (Mt 16:16 // Mk 8:29 // Lk 9:20), she multiplies titles in what is, in the opinion of Schneiders (1987b:53), 'the most fully developed confession of Johannine faith in the Fourth Gospel.' Thus does Martha enter into eternal life.

---

4 In the light of our commentary on 11:22-25, it should be more understandable why John highlights the necessity of Jesus' departure from the world (see 14:1-4; 16:5-8,28; 17:11,13).

Third dialogue: Jesus and Mary (11:28-32)

> [28] When she had said this, she went and called her sister Mary secretly, saying, 'The teacher is here and is asking for you.' [29] As soon as she heard this, she rose quickly and went to him. [30] For Jesus had not yet come into the village, but was still where Martha had met him. [31] So when the Jews who were with her in the house comforting her saw Mary get up quickly and go out, they followed her, presuming that she was going to the tomb to weep there. [32] When Mary came to where Jesus was and saw him, she fell at his feet and said to him, 'Lord, if you had been here, my brother would not have died.'

We can only conjecture why Jesus asks to see Mary. Why does he not wait until he reaches the village? And why does Martha issue Jesus' invitation to her sister secretly? The title 'teacher', as Marsh (1968:432) remarks: 'seems oddly mundane after the exalted titles used by Martha'.

Presumably unaware of the conversation her sister has had with Jesus, Mary, ever responsive to his voice, goes out with uncharacteristic haste to meet him and falls at his feet (cf. Mt 9:18 and parallels — Jairus). The scene is reminiscent of a happier occasion at Bethany, recorded by Luke, when Mary chose 'the better part' (Lk 10:38-42).

Sharing Martha's trust in their friend, she repeats what her sister said to Jesus (sentiments they had probably expressed to one another many times while awaiting his arrival): 'Lord, if you had been here, my brother would not have died' (11:32; cf. 11:21).

Fourth Dialogue: Jesus and the Jews (11:33-37)

> [33] When Jesus saw her weeping and the Jews who had come with her weeping, he became perturbed and deeply troubled, [34] and said, 'Where have you laid him?' They said to him, 'Sir, come and see.' [35] And Jesus wept. [36] So

the Jews said, 'See how he loved him.' ³⁷But some of them said, 'Could not the one who opened the eyes of the blind man have done something so that this man would not have died?'

The sight of Mary weeping at the tomb of the beloved Lazarus is a profoundly moving experience for Jesus, the complexity of which is not easily captured in translations from the Greek original. The New American Bible (revised New Testament, 1986) says that he becomes 'perturbed and deeply troubled' (cf. 11:38), while Marsh (1968:433) suggests that 'deeply resentful in spirit' would be an acceptable translation.

Jesus is grief stricken at the loss of a dear friend; but it is also possible that, confronted with the awful reality of death, he is painfully aware of what may soon befall him at the hands of his enemies. With this possibility in mind, McGann (1988:134) writes: 'Taken all in all, one could wonder if this is not John's version of Gethsemani where Jesus in the presence of Lazarus has to do battle with his own oncoming death.'

Jesus asks the mourners who accompany Mary, 'Where have you laid him?' It is a question that will have its echo in the query of another grieving Mary at another tomb — his own (20:2,13,15). The Jews reply, 'Sir, come and see' (cf. 1:39; 1:46; 4:29).

Then the one who will wipe away every tear from our eyes (Rev 21:4) weeps copiously — tears of compassion and, I believe, tears of horror at the prospect of his own confrontation with the 'last enemy'. In the words of Schneiders (1987b:54), 'Jesus, in his most fully human moment in the Fourth Gospel, legitimates human agony in the face of death.'

There is a certain irony in the Jews' remark, 'See how he loved him.' They do not appreciate the depth of Jesus' love either for Lazarus or for all people (themselves included) for whom he will soon die a shameful death. 'No one has greater love than this, to lay down one's life for one's friends' (15:13; cf. 13:1).

With another of his many cross-references, the writer has some of those present ask, 'Could not the one who opened the eyes of the blind man have done something so that this man would not have died?' The disciples may well have asked just such a question before Jesus set out for Bethany; and we ourselves may have asked our version of it many times.

Fifth dialogue: Jesus and Martha (11:38-41)

> 38So Jesus, perturbed again, came to the tomb. It was a cave, and a stone lay across it. 39Jesus said, 'Take away the stone.' Martha, the dead man's sister, said to him, 'Lord, by now there will be a stench; he has been dead for four days.' 40Jesus said to her, 'Did I not tell you that if you believe you will see the glory of God?' 41So they took away the stone. ...

What a doleful spectacle we find at the tomb of Lazarus who, according to common practice, has been interred in a cave sealed by a heavy stone. It is a place of darkness and imprisonment. There are no grounds for hope, humanly speaking; and Jesus once again, we are told, gives vent to his emotions.

However, as always in this Gospel, he is in control of the situation.[5] He orders the bystanders to remove the stone from the entrance to the tomb. Martha, who still cannot see that her brother can rise *now*, reacts by telling

---

[5] Keep in mind that the Christology of the Fourth Gospel is what is sometimes called a 'high' Christology. We may presume that, in the historical circumstances of his daily life, Jesus was not always supremely in control. John's portrait of him is theological.

Jesus that, after four days, corruption will have invaded the remains.

Recalling what he said to her earlier, Jesus replies, 'Did I not tell you that if you believe you will see the glory of God?' (11:40; cf. 11:23-26). As we have already noted, faith and glory are closely related themes in this chapter (cf. 11:4).

Whatever she or the others present make of these words, we do not know; but, as he speaks like one with authority, they do his bidding and roll back the stone.

Sixth dialogue: Jesus and the Father (11:41-42)

> [41]... And Jesus raised his eyes and said, 'Father, I thank you for hearing me. [42]I know that you always hear me; but because of the crowd here I have said this, that they may believe that you sent me.'

Using a traditionally prayerful gesture (cf. 17:1), Jesus raises his eyes and addresses his Father. Apart from the multiplication of the loaves (6:11; Mt 14:19 and parallels), this is the only time when it is related that Jesus prays before a miracle. On both occasions it is a prayer of thanksgiving, not a prayer requesting a miracle.

Jesus prays for the benefit of those present in the hope that they may correctly read the sign he is about to perform and come to a position of faith (cf. 11:15; 20:31). As with all of his signs, the raising of Lazarus is intended to point to the Father whose glory he reveals and on whose authority he acts (5:30).

Seventh dialogue: Jesus and Lazarus (11:43-44)

> [43]And when he said this, he cried out in a loud voice, 'Lazarus, come out!' [44]The dead man came out, tied hand and foot with burial bands, and his face was

Day Four

wrapped in a cloth. So Jesus said to them, 'Untie him and let him go.'

In this final highly dramatic scene, we have the climax not only of this story but also of all Jesus' sign activity in the Fourth Gospel. The most telling example of the life-giving word of Jesus in the Christian Scriptures (cf. 4:50,51,53), the restoration of life to Lazarus anticipates the fulfilment of his prophecy, '... the hour is coming in which all who are in the tombs will hear his voice' (5:28).

'Lazarus, come out!' he cries out in a voice that, as a familiar English idiom expresses it, would awaken the dead. Such loudness of utterance is suggestive of power and confidence.

Lazarus, obedient to the word of his Lord, emerges from the tomb; but, whereas Jesus will leave his wrappings and face veil behind (20:4-7), Lazarus comes forth 'tied hand and foot with burial bands, and his face ... wrapped in a cloth'. The contrast is surely deliberate. Jesus is bound by his captors in the garden (18:12) and by those who conduct his burial (19:40); but, in his resurrection, he is supremely free.

Jesus' third and final command is, 'Untie him and let him go.' As he often does, he involves those present in the saving action.

His prayer to the Father (11:42) is answered and the worst fears of his enemies are realised (see 11:48; 12:19); for 'many of the Jews who had come to Mary and seen what he had done began to believe in him' (11:45).

How ironical it is that some of the Pharisees and chief priests respond to this sign by convening the Sanhedrin (11:47). Jesus reveals himself as 'the author of life' (Acts 3:15); yet from that day on they plan to kill him (11:53).

2. The Anointing at Bethany (12:1-11)

¹Six days before Passover Jesus came to Bethany, where Lazarus was, whom Jesus had raised from the dead. ²They gave a dinner for him there, and Martha served, while Lazarus was one of those reclining at table with him. ³Mary took a liter of costly perfumed oil made from genuine aromatic nard and anointed the feet of Jesus and dried them with her hair; the house was filled with the fragrance of the oil. ⁴Then Judas the Iscariot, one [of] his disciples, and the one who would betray him, said, ⁵'Why was this oil not sold for three hundred days' wages and given to the poor?' ⁶He said this not because he cared about the poor but because he was a thief and held the money bag and used to steal the contributions. ⁷So Jesus said, 'Leave her alone. Let her keep this for the day of my burial. ⁸You always have the poor with you, but you do not always have me.' ⁹[The] large crowd of the Jews found out that he was there and came, not only because of Jesus, but also to see Lazarus, whom he had raised from the dead. ¹⁰And the chief priests plotted to kill Lazarus too, ¹¹because many of the Jews were turning away and believing in Jesus because of him.

In John's Gospel the banquet at Bethany takes place six days before Jesus goes up to Jerusalem for the Passover celebration, whereas in both the Matthean and Marcan versions it occurs after Jesus' entry into Jerusalem and just two days before the Passover (Mt 26:6-13 // Mk 14:3-9). Luke adapts what is probably a common tradition to his own purpose, making no reference to Bethany and situating the anointing in a different context without direct reference to the events of Jesus' passion and death (Lk 7:36-50). A study of the four versions in parallel columns would reveal significant similarities and differences of detail.

In the very first verse John ties his narrative of the anointing to the events of the raising of Lazarus from the dead; and he concludes it on an ominous note with a reference to the plot of the chief priests to kill Lazarus as well as Jesus. The shadow of the cross falls across this scene of domestic conviviality.

While Lazarus reclines at table with Jesus as another 'beloved disciple' will do at the farewell supper (13:25; 21:20), Martha, in her customary role (cf. Lk 10:40), attends to the serving. Her sister Mary falls at Jesus' feet (cf. 11:32; Lk 10:39), expressing her faith not in words but in personal ministrations lovingly performed.

In a gesture which far surpasses the usual hospitality extended to a guest, she anoints Jesus' feet (cf. Lk 7:38) with 'costly perfumed oil' and dries them with her hair, with the result that the whole house is filled with the fragrance of the ointment.

In Matthew and Mark, the woman in the house of Simon the leper at Bethany anoints Jesus' head (Mt 26:7 // Mk 14:3) — a not uncommon act of courtesy at a banquet (cf. Lk 7:46). Why then does John opt for the anointing of Jesus' feet? After all, he does appear to be familiar with the Marcan details of 'perfumed oil, costly genuine spikenard' (Mk 14:3) valued at 'more than 300 days' wages' (Mk 14:5).

Perhaps John thought his version to be more expressive of his theological concern with the burial of the crucified Jesus, in preparation for which the whole body of the Saviour will be anointed in similarly extravagant fashion (19:39-40).

In passing, we may note that the woman in the Lucan story also dries Jesus' feet with her hair (Lk 7:38) — a detail not mentioned by Matthew or Mark.[6]

---

[6] The popular image of the woman in Luke 7:36-50 as a penitent sinner can obscure the fact that she is possessed of greater insight than Simon the Pharisee with respect to the identity of Jesus. Jesus acknowledges her as a woman of faith (Lk 7:50).

Mary's gesture does not meet with universal approval. Judas Iscariot, the keeper of the purse who will betray Jesus, says: 'Why was this oil not sold for three hundred days' wages and given to the poor?' It is significant that John, who alone among the evangelists describes him as 'a thief', identifies the complainant as Judas; for in this way he links the story even more closely with the death of Jesus. Matthew attributes the complaint to 'the disciples' (Mt 26:8) and Mark to 'some who were indignant' (Mk 14:4).

Jesus comes to Mary's defence. 'Leave her alone,' he says. 'Let her keep this for the day of my burial' (12:7; cf. Mt 26:12; Mk 14:8). 'You have the poor always with you,' he continues, 'but you do not always have me.' On this somewhat difficult verse, Marsh (1968:456-457) comments:

> To bear witness to the unique significance of the death and resurrection of Jesus in contemporary action is something that must be done now, or not at all. Service to the poor, or any other general care for humanity, is a continuing obligation for Christian people.

As the episode concludes, a 'large crowd' appears on the scene, anxious to see Jesus and the man who came back from the dead. Their enthusiasm attracts the disfavour of the chief priests who plot to kill not only Jesus (cf. 11:53) but Lazarus as well.

Another crowd will be much in evidence on the following day (12:12) when Jesus makes his triumphal entry into the city of Jerusalem and again later when he treads his weary way to Calvary and the glory of the cross.

2. PRAYING WITH LAZARUS

At first glance it may seem somewhat unusual to identify with a character who says nothing and does little in the only episode of the Gospel in which he appears. Would

Day Four

it not be better and more in keeping with the theme of faith, which has been so central to our reflections over the past few days, to pray imaginatively from the perspective of Mary who exemplifies faith or of Martha who confesses Jesus as the Messiah?

This may be so; and the retreatant should feel completely free to stand in the shoes of Martha or Mary instead. However, since faith and life are closely related themes in the Fourth Gospel, there may be good, if not immediately obvious, reasons to recommend the rather sobering exercise of identifying with the man whom Jesus raises from the realm of the dead.

This need not necessarily entail anything as graphic as the visualisation of the nine stages of the decomposition of one's own corpse which one of the Buddhist 'reality meditations' calls for. That is up to the individual retreatant.

Begin on a happier note in the dwelling of the beloved family at Bethany in the presence of Jesus. This has been a place of refuge from his enemies and of solace for him in his trials and disappointments. He, who sometimes 'has nowhere to rest his head' (Mt 8:20 // Lk 9:58), is at home here. Among friends, he pours out his heart and shares his joys, his hopes and his fears.

Return to this same place four days after the death of Lazarus. Everyone is in mourning as Jesus and his disciples arrive from the other Bethany across the Jordan where John first baptised (cf. 1:28; 10:40). He enters into dialogue first with Martha and then with Mary.

Having taken in this sorrowful situation as a spectator rather than as a participant, join Lazarus in the tomb. If you are comfortable with the idea, lie on the floor with your eyes closed and your hands by your side. Become aware of the encompassing darkness and the musty smell of earth. Feel the constriction of the burial bands that bind you in this silent place beyond the reach of those who loved you in life.

There comes to you, you know not how, the grinding noise of the stone as it is rolled away from the entrance to the tomb. Above the babble of the bystanders, you hear a once familiar voice call in stentorian tones, 'Lazarus, come out!' Like an echo the command resonates in your restored consciousness. Listen as you hear it repeated over and over, addressing first Lazarus and then yourself personally by name.

Stand upright gradually and, with your eyes still closed and your body still bound, walk very slowly out of the tomb in the direction of Jesus. At his further command, eager hands release you and your eyes open to the vision of Jesus and your beloved sisters, Mary and Martha.

What are your thoughts and feelings as you walk home with them? Once the erstwhile mourners and the curious visitors have departed, what transpires in the happy hours you share together? The last prayerful words of Lazarus for the day might well be: 'O LORD, you brought me up from the nether world; you preserved me from among those going down into the pit' (Ps 31:4).

3. PRAYING WITH JESUS

We must never lose sight of the fact that the historical Jesus, who is like us in all but sin (cf. Heb 4:15), prays out of a deeply felt human need to praise and thank God and to make intercession both for himself and for those to whom he ministers. To suggest otherwise is to reduce Jesus' prayer to pious play-acting.

His prayers reveal his vulnerability, his remarkable capacity for empathy with the afflicted, and his exquisite sensitivity to people to whom he is attached by emotional ties or by bonds of friendship. All of these qualities are

Day Four

in evidence in the passages which tell of the raising of Lazarus and the ministrations of Mary at the dinner table.

In this session you are invited to watch and pray with Jesus as he casts his mind back over these highly significant events and as he looks forward to those which, in the theology of the evangelist, they prefigure. As immediate preparation for this imaginative meditation, please read the remainder of chapter 12 — that is, 12:12-50.

In the quiet of the evening, let us now walk across the Kidron valley with Jesus to the garden on the Mount of Olives where he and his disciples have been accustomed to gather (cf. Jn 18:2). It is the evening of that tumultuous day after the banquet at Bethany. He has been welcomed to Jerusalem by an enthusiastic crowd who have heard of the raising of Lazarus; he has spoken to the Greek friends of Philip about the arrival of his hour, about death yielding place to life and about his being 'lifted up from the earth'.

Jesus' sentiments at this time of prayer are, we may reasonably surmise, in harmony with the following words of the Psalmist. Let us pray them slowly with Jesus, pausing occasionally for reflection as the Spirit moves:

> I bless the LORD who counsels me;
> even in the night my heart exhorts me.
> I set the LORD ever before me;
> with him at my right hand I shall not be disturbed.
> Therefore my heart is glad and my soul rejoices,
> my body, too, abides, in confidence;
> Because you will not abandon my soul to the nether world,
> nor will you suffer your faithful one to undergo corruption.
> You will show me the path of life,
> fullness of joys in your presence,
> the delights at your right hand forever (Ps 16:7-11).

Another prayer from the Psalter (Jesus' own prayer book) which is very much to the point is Psalm 27 (refer to your Bible).

4. CONTEXTUAL PRAYER

Among the many possible subjects for contextual prayer that today's readings open up, there is probably none more basic than our strongly felt need to be called forth to newness of life from the bondage (often self-imposed) which impedes our growth as human beings. We desire to be liberated from the shackles that prevent us from realising our own truth and thus attaining that authentic selfhood which, in Christian terms, we would call holiness.

Some of these impediments are internal to the human psyche and, in large measure, reflect our failure to attune our will to the will of God. Unfortunately, we cannot say with Jesus, 'I always do what is pleasing to him' (8:29). Others derive from the social environment in which we live and take a variety of forms which we may subsume under the heading of dehumanising structures. Each of us will have his or her own preferred list based on personal experience.

Ultimately, the only freedom that will satisfy the yearning of our restless hearts for abundant life is what Paul terms 'the glorious freedom of the children of God' (Rom 8:21; cf. Jn 1:12; 1 Jn 3:1-2). It is the fruit of loving communion with God and with one another. As John expresses it: 'We know that we have passed from death to life because we love our brothers. Whoever does not love remains in death' (1 Jn 3:14-16; cf. 4:7-11).

Jesus, who took upon himself the consequences of our loss of freedom, is nonetheless the supremely and radically free human being; for he is the living embodiment of the liberating truth he proclaims (cf. 8:32; 14:6). His life-giving mission, which embraces all people and the whole person, confronts all forms of slavery.

With faith and hope in him, let us ask for deliverance from whatever it is that enslaves us: sinful habits; inordinate attachment to power, property or prestige; irrational guilt

Day Four

and scruples; legalism; prejudice in any of its unlovely manifestations (racial, religious, social class); et cetera.

Paul offers us good advice which we would do well to heed during this time of retreat: 'For freedom Christ set us free; so stand firm and do not submit again to the yoke of slavery' (Gal 5:1).

Finally, lest our prayer be selfishly restricted to our own personal concerns, let us also be mindful of our sisters and brothers in so many parts of the world whose human rights are not respected and whose basic freedoms are exercised only with the greatest difficulty. Our action on their behalf will make our prayer for them more credible.

5. PRAYING THE MANTRA

As on the other days, choose a mantra which expresses the hopes and aspirations which have been enkindled in you as a result of your prayerful reflection on the prescribed texts. The following suggestions may be helpful now or on some future occasion when you return to the story of the beloved family of Bethany: 'You are the resurrection and the life' (cf. 11:25); 'Lord, take away the stone' (cf. 11:39); 'See how he loves me' (cf. 11:36); or simply, 'Jesus wept' (11:35).

DAY FIVE

JESUS AND A TRIO OF DISCIPLES
JUDAS, PETER, THOMAS

1. REFLECTIVE STUDY OF THE TEXT

Introduction

Only rather belatedly has St John's Gospel been acknowledged as a fertile area for New Testament studies on the nature and character of Christian discipleship. This is surprising in view of the fact that the word for disciple (Gk *mathētēs*) occurs more often in John than in any of the Synoptic Gospels or in the Acts of the Apostles.[1]

Allowing for differences of theological emphasis, a study of these books reveals that Christian discipleship is basically a response of faith to a call in which Jesus takes the initiative. It finds expression in commitment to his person, obedient witness to his teaching, and a willingness to share in his saving ministry as a partner in service.

John frequently speaks of it in terms of following Jesus (1:37,38,40,43; 8:12; 10:4,5,27; 12:26; 13:36,37; 18:15; 21:19). However, the three texts which best encapsulate the Johannine teaching on discipleship are as follows: 8:31; 13:35; and 15:1-17 — Jesus' discourse on the vine and the branches.

---

1 Segovia (1985:95, n.6) gives the following statistics: Mt 73x; Mk 46x; Lk 37x; Jn 78x; Acts 28x.

By way of preparation for this day of reflection, the retreatant is advised to read and to dwell prayerfully upon these three texts. The scriptural passages prescribed for today can be read aloud later in conjunction with the commentaries on them; they need not be read twice as on previous days.

Preliminary observations

All three Synoptic Gospels record the call and missioning by Jesus of a select group of twelve men from a larger body of disciples (see Mt 10:1-4 // Mk 3:13-19 // Lk 6:12-16). He himself designated them 'apostles' (Lk 6:13). Apart from Peter, the sons of Zebedee, and Judas Iscariot, the writers do not tell us much about them as individuals, preferring to treat them collectively as an important institution which, in view of the twelve tribes of the old dispensation, has a symbolic character (Mt 19:28; Lk 22:30).

John, though he does refer to 'the Twelve' in a few places (6:67,70-71; 20:24), apparently sees no reason to include a list of them. He mentions by name only the following: Andrew, Peter, Philip, Nathanael (Bartholomew?), Thomas and Judas Iscariot. In addition, he accords a special place of honour to a seventh follower of Jesus whom he calls the 'beloved disciple' and whom tradition has identified (not necessarily correctly) with John the Apostle.

A number of these disciples (John never calls them 'apostles') feature much more prominently in the Fourth Gospel than they do in the Synoptic writings. For purposes of this reflection, we will consider in detail the 'adventures in grace' of three of them — Judas, Peter, and Thomas.

In view of the amount of material which is presented below, it would be well for the retreatant to limit his or her attention, according to perceived personal spiritual needs, to no more than two of these disciples. My suggestion is that you focus on Judas and either Peter or Thomas. Note that guidelines for prayer will be given only with reference to Peter.

The justification for including the Judas story for reflection, if not as the basis of imaginative prayer, lies in the fact that it provides a useful contrast to the eventual fidelity of the other two disciples. Moreover, as McNamara (1983:19) notes: 'In the spiritual life it is as important to be in touch with your capacity for evil as it is to be in touch with your capacity for good.'

1. Judas (Jn 6:70-71; 12:1-8; 13:2,21-30; 18:2-5)

Introduction

Of all the characters we meet in John's Gospel, Judas Iscariot is probably the one we find most distasteful; and yet, conscious of our own sinfulness, we know full well that we cannot observe his story from a distance.

With this in mind, Harper (1986), in an article arrestingly entitled 'Judas, Our Brother', points out the appropriateness of Bach's choice (contrary to previous practice) of the chorus rather than a soloist to sing the words, 'Is it I, Lord?', in his *St Matthew's Passion*.

For his part, another creative genius sees fit to pass a much more severe judgment on this disciple turned traitor. In Book XXXIV of the *Inferno*, Dante takes us to the lowest and coldest pit of hell which he depicts as a vast frozen lake made up of the tears of humankind. It is the abode of Satan — a hideous three-headed monster who holds in his mouths to left and right the two disturbers of the civil order, Brutus and Cassius. Between them, in the jaws of the evil one, is the unfortunate Judas.

It is a ghastly image; but, as we may need to remind ourselves, it is not up to us to pass judgment on Judas or, for that matter, on anyone else. My own belief and hope is that the last word in the Judas story is uttered by Jesus himself when, hanging on the cross between two criminals (Lk 23:33) or revolutionaries (Mt 27:38 // Mk 15:27), he says, 'Father, forgive them, they know not what they do' (Lk 23:34).

If Jesus died on account of Judas, he also died **for** him.

Who is Judas Iscariot?

If, as his name suggests, Judas is of the land and tribe of Judah, he is a person who can be justly proud of a rich heritage. He is the son of Simon the Iscariot (6:71; 13:2,26; cf. 12:4), a descendant of those people who were taken off into captivity in Babylon and who, unlike the despised Samaritans, remained faithful to their God.

Called by Jesus as 'one of the Twelve' (6:71), he has been entrusted with the common purse (12:6) and is apparently respected among his peers who do not suspect him when Jesus speaks about a betrayer in their midst. 'The disciples looked at one another,' we are told, 'at a loss as to whom he meant' (13:22). Peter asks the beloved disciple, who occupies a place of privilege, to find out (13:23-24).

As a Judean, Judas is an 'outsider' among Jesus and his closest disciples, all of whom (most probably) come from Galilee. Jesus himself is from the rather insignificant town of Nazareth (1:45-46); Nathanael is a native of Cana (21:2); and Philip, Peter and Andrew hail from Bethsaida (1:44).[2]

In passing, we may note that Jesus feels welcome in Galilee not only because it is his home province but also

---

[2] See also with reference to Peter: Mt 26:73 // Mk 14:70 // Lk 22:59.

because of the reception he receives there (4:45). It is in Judea that his teaching is rejected and that his life is threatened on more than one occasion (7:1; 8:59; 10:31,39).

Judas: the Johannine portrait

All the Gospels record the call of Peter (Mt 4:18-20 // Mk 1:16-18; cf. Lk 5:1-11), the disciple who denies his master; but none of the evangelists sees fit to relate the events surrounding the call of Judas. He is, however, named in all the Synoptic lists of the twelve apostles — significantly in the last place each time (Mt 10:2-4; Mk 3:16-19; Lk 6:14-16).

In these lists he is identified as a 'betrayer' (Mt 10:4; Mk 3:19) or as a 'traitor' (Lk 6:16); but it is John who is least sympathetic, even harsh, in his portrayal of Judas. He presents him (particularly to the potential recidivists in his own community, we may suppose) as a representative figure of those 'disciples [of Jesus who] returned to their former way of life and no longer accompanied him' (6:66).

John reminds us frequently of Judas's perfidy (see 6:64,70-71; 12:4; 13:21; 18:2,5); and, going a step further than the other evangelists, he has Jesus speak of him as 'a devil' (6:70; cf. 1 Jn 3:8-10). For him, Judas is a creature of the night (13:30; cf. 18:3), a backslider into whose faithless heart Satan makes entry (13:2,27; cf. 8:41,44; Lk 22:3) just as surely as Jesus and his Father enter into the hearts of those disciples who remain faithful (14:20,23; cf. 17:21,23,26).

Furthermore, in the anointing scene, John alone among the evangelists mentions Judas by name as the one who protests at Jesus' ready acceptance of the extravagant gesture of the ministering woman (12:4-5). Matthew, on the other hand, has 'the disciples' ask, 'Why this waste?'

(Mt 26:8); and Mark attributes the intervention to 'some who were indignant' (Mk 14:4).

John proceeds to identify Judas as 'a thief' (12:6); but, unlike the Synoptic writers (Mt 26:15 // Mk 14:11 // Lk 22:5), he nowhere suggests that it is for money that Judas betrays his master. There is no record in the Fourth Gospel of 'the wages of his iniquity' (Acts 1:18), of the 30 pieces of silver of which Matthew speaks (26:15; 27:3,9); and equally notable by its absence is any reference to Judas's remorse (Mt 27:3-5).

It is in the context of another meal, the last supper that Jesus takes with 'his own' (13:1), that we find the most damning indictment of Judas in John's Gospel. Addressing his Father, Jesus prays: 'When I was with them I protected them in your name that you gave me, and I guarded them, and none of them was lost except the son of destruction, in order that the scripture might be fulfilled' (17:12). The Greek phrase which is here rendered 'son of destruction' is also used by Paul in his second letter to the Thessalonians where it identifies the Antichrist (2 Thess 2:3).

This description of Judas is all the more poignant when we consider the respectful intimacy of Jesus' gesture of handing him a morsel of food dipped in the common dish (13:26). The ease of this interaction and the private nature of Jesus' remark to him may suggest that Judas is reclining at table as close to the Lord as the beloved disciple is (cf. 13:23-25).

With good reason does Jesus recall the words of the Psalmist: 'Even my friend who had my trust and partook of my bread, has raised his heal against me' (Ps 41:10; cf. Jn 13:18). Judas accepts the morsel but he rejects the 'living bread that came down from heaven' (6:51). He forsakes the 'light of life' (8:12; cf. 9:5, 11:9; 1 Jn 1:5-7) and disappears into the darkness of sin and death.

After Jesus and his other disciples have also gone forth from the supper room to the garden across the Kidron Valley (18:1), we meet Judas for the last time (18:2,5). It is fully in keeping with the Christology of the Fourth Gospel that he says nothing and does nothing on this occasion.

There is no place for the traitor's kiss in the Johannine scheme of things (cf. Mt 26:48-49 // Mk 14:44-45 // Lk 22:47-48); for Jesus is always in control of the situation. This is not the garden of the agony, as in the Synoptic writings (cf. Mt 26:36-46 // Mk 14:32-42 // Lk 22:40-46), but the place where Jesus' glory is revealed. He takes the initiative; and, as he utters the divine name ('I AM' — 18:5,8), the minions of earthly power fall at his feet (18:6).

Wherein lies the tragedy of Judas?

The theme of the rejection of Jesus is introduced into the Gospel as early as the prologue. 'He came to what was his own, but his own people did not accept him' (1:11). Even his own chosen disciples (with one notable exception) desert him in his time of need, and Peter denies him three times; but of Judas alone is it stated that he betrays him.

These two men, Peter and Judas, are the only ones mentioned by name in that extraordinary scene (peculiar to John) in which Jesus washes the feet of his disciples (13:1-12). Their stories, so different in their outcome, invite comparison. The weakness of both men is clearly exposed by the evangelist; but, in the mystery of human existence graced by the presence of God, Judas has the experience but misses the meaning. Where Peter finds faith, he loses hope.

Other contrasts are also possible. Unlike the man born blind who comes to a knowledge of the truth (9:1-41),

Judas dies blind to the only truth that has the power to set him free. Unlike the many people of faith who bring their friends to Jesus, Judas, in his infidelity, brings only the enemy (18:3).

Some people may see in Judas a tragic hero in the Shakespearean sense — a great but flawed man who becomes belatedly and painfully aware of his part in the havoc that surrounds him. Others may see in him but a wasted and unfortunate life that exemplifies 'the banality of evil' — a pathetic existence in which everything is filtered through the prism of self-interest.

For me, Judas emerges from the pages of the Fourth Gospel as a realist and as a pragmatist. He was right in asserting that Mary of Bethany's act of anointing Jesus' feet was extravagant; the poor could have benefited from the 'three hundred days' wages' (12:5) spent on the costly oil. Had not Jesus himself constantly displayed much concern and solicitude for the poor and outcast? Was not such compassion the standard by which all would some day be judged (cf. Mt 25:31-46)?

However, his undoing probably lies in the fact that he was also an idealist with an agenda quite at variance with that of Jesus who seeks to do his Father's will in all things (cf. 4:34). While we can only guess at his motives, I believe that Judas's aspirations are best summed up in the statement of the two disciples who meet Jesus Risen on the way to Emmaus: 'But we were hoping that he would be the one to redeem Israel' (Lk 24:21).

Judas's commitment to Jesus could not sustain the realisation that he was being called to follow a suffering Messiah (Mt 16:21 // Mk 8:31 // Lk 9:22), devoid of political ambition, whose disciples would share in his ignominy (15:18-20; cf. Mt 16:24-25 // Mk 8:34-35 // Lk 9:23-24). To resolve this crisis he chose to turn from the Way which is Christ and to tread the lonely path of betrayal.

2. Peter *(Jn 1:40-42; 6:66-69; 13:6-9, 24, 36-38; 18:10-11,15-18, 25-27; 20:2-10; 21:1-23)*

Introduction

As with Nicodemus, we must distinguish between Peter's role in the Fourth Gospel and his relevance to the Johannine community. His frequent appearances in the Gospel reveal both the complexity of his character and the difficulties that confront many would-be disciples of Jesus the Nazarene. In this sense, Peter is a representative figure from whom the community of the evangelist had much to learn. However, he appears to have been less important to this community as a person than the 'beloved disciple'.

In the passages where Peter and the beloved disciple appear together (13:21-26; 18:15-18; 20:2-10; 21:20-24), the juxtaposition usually serves to reveal the superior status and greater insight of the latter. The beloved disciple is the one who reclines in the place of honour by Jesus at the table (13:25); he is the one who comprehends the significance of the empty tomb (20:8) and who recognises the man on the beach as his risen Lord (21:7). Moreover, on the good assumption that he is the unnamed disciple who accompanies Peter to the house of Annas, it is because he is 'the acquaintance of the high priest' (18:16) that he is able to help Peter gain entry to the courtyard where he thrice denies that he is Jesus' disciple.

It is true that chapter 21 highlights the importance of Peter among the disciples; but this is a later redactional addition, probably designed to harmonise this Gospel with the Synoptic writings. It should be read in conjunction with Lk 5:1-11 (the miraculous catch of fish) and Mt 16:13-20 (the conferment of leadership on Peter).

The call of Peter (1:40-42)

In keeping with the missionary character of Johannine faith, it is Andrew, the former disciple of John the Baptist (1:35,40), who leads his brother, Simon Peter, to Jesus. 'We have found the Messiah,' he tells him (1:41; cf. 11:27).

Peter is not, contrary to what we read in the Synoptic accounts (Mt 4:18 // Mk 1:16; cf. Lk 5:1-11), the first mentioned of those called by Jesus. At the beginning of the Fourth Gospel, he is placed among rather than at the head of the disciples (contrast 21:2).

The Greek text suggests that Jesus looks intently at Peter in this, their first meeting. He will do so again in less happy circumstances following Peter's threefold denial (Lk 22:61). It is the penetrating gaze of one who speaks as if he already knows all there is to be known about the fisherman (21:3) from Bethsaida (1:44). He will display similar superior knowledge in his interchange with Nathanael (1:47-50).

'You are Simon the son of John; you will be called Kephas,' he says to him. The change of name is important, the more so as this is the only time Jesus confers a new name on anyone. As with Abraham (Gen 17:5) and Jacob (Gen 32:28-29) in the Hebrew Scriptures, it signifies a new relationship with God.

Given that 'Kephas' is the Greek transliteration of the Aramaic* word for 'rock', this incident recalls the event in Matthew's Gospel in which Peter, having acknowledged Jesus as 'the Messiah, the Son of the living God' (Mt 16:16), is told by Jesus: 'Blessed are you, Simon son of Jonah ... you are Peter, and upon this rock I will build my church ... (Mt 16:17-18; cf. Mt 10:2 // Mk 3:16 // Lk 6:14).

Day Five

A confession of faith (6:68-69)

John does not follow a strict chronological sequence in the presentation of his material; so we can only conjecture what experiences Peter may have had by the time we meet him again after the multiplication of the loaves. We cannot assume that he has witnessed the Cana sign (2:1-12) or the cleansing of the Temple (2:13-25) or that he has travelled with Jesus through Samaria (4:1-42).

In the synagogue of Capernaum (6:59), many of the disciples find Jesus' discourse about the bread of life unpalatable. 'This saying is hard; who can accept it?' they say (6:60). He is aware of their murmuring, knowing 'from the beginning the ones who would not believe and the one who would betray him' (6:64).

The ominous note which is struck in this episode doubtless reflects the concern of the writer for the falling away from faith that he had to contend with in his own community. Jesus' question, 'Do you also want to leave?' (6:67), is addressed not only to the Twelve but also to the Johannine church.

Peter's confession (it is peculiar to the Fourth Gospel) is the one that John would have potential defectors from his own community take to heart. 'Master, to whom shall we go? You have the words of eternal life. We have come to believe and are convinced that you are the Holy One of God' (6:68-69; cf. Mk 1:24 // Lk 4:34).

The same Peter, who readily accepts the lifegiving words which others consider too difficult, will later find it impossible to admit that he is one of Jesus' disciples (18:17, 25,27). His failure then will demonstrate not only a lack of courage but a total incomprehension of how this 'Holy One of God' could permit himself to be treated so ignominiously.

It is interesting to note that Peter's confession of Jesus in the Synoptic Gospels (also in response to a question) as 'the Messiah, the Son of the living God' (Mt 16:16; cf. Mk 8:29; Lk 9:20) is placed on the lips of Martha of Bethany in this Gospel (11:27).

The washing of Peter's feet (13:6-9)

Like so many of the sign-events in John's Gospel, the washing of the disciples' feet does not have a single, univocal meaning. It can be seen, as I have pointed out in another reflection (Grenier 1989) in a number of ways: as an act of exemplary humility; as a model of servant leadership; as an act which is revelatory, parabolic and judgmental; as a prophetic act which (like the institution of the Eucharist in the Synoptic Gospels) proleptically* reveals the saving character of Jesus' death; and, in Hultgren's (1982:542) terminology, as 'a symbolic act of eschatological* hospitality'. Because of time and space constraints, our concern here will be only with Peter's part in this quite unprecedented inversion of the master-servant relationship.

He alone of all the disciples protests at the menial service that Jesus is about to perform for him. 'Master, are you going to wash my feet?' he asks in complete disbelief and bewilderment. Jesus reassures him by saying, 'What I am doing, you do not understand now, but you will understand later.' Far from convinced, Peter retorts with some vehemence, 'You will never wash my feet.'

He changes his tune, however, when Jesus answers him bluntly, 'Unless I wash you, you will have no inheritance with me.' At this, Peter replies in typically extravagant fashion, 'Master, then not only my feet, but my hands and head as well.'

Deep down Peter realises that, by being amenable to Jesus' suggestion that he should have his feet washed, his whole world will be turned upside down, with the result

Day Five

that he will have to make significant changes in his own way of relating to people. To quote Schneiders (1981:83): 'In some way, Peter grasped that complicity in this act involved acceptance of a radical reinterpretation of his own lifeworld, a genuine conversion of some kind which he was not prepared to undergo.'

Eventually, the reluctant Peter will come to appreciate the meaning of what Jesus does in this gesture of self-emptying (cf. Phil 2:7). In his first epistle he may well be alluding to this experience when he writes, 'And most of all you must put on the apron of humility, to serve one another' (1 Pet 5:5 — TEV).

The prediction of Peter's denial (13:36-38)

Before the conclusion of this memorable meal, Jesus announces his imminent betrayal by Judas (13:21-30); he proclaims the 'new commandment' of love (13:34) of which he has just given such a striking example; and he predicts with painful insight Peter's triple denial (13:36-38). With good dramatic effect the evangelist prepares us for the events that are yet to come.

The arrest of Jesus: Peter's intervention (18:10-11)

All four evangelists portray Peter as an impulsive man who declares himself willing to stand by Jesus come what may (Mt 26:33-35 // Mk 14:29-31 // Lk 22:33-34; Jn 13:36-38). The account in Matthew of his stepping out of the boat, when Jesus bids him walk across the waters, supports this assertion (Mt 14:28-31; cf. Jn 21:7).

Very much in character, therefore, is Peter's action in the garden when Jesus is arrested. In the presence of Judas and a large band of armed Roman soldiers (18:2-3), he unsheathes his sword and strikes Malchus, 'the high priest's slave', a vicious blow on the head, severing his right ear (18:10). John alone identifies the wielder of the sword and his victim (cf. Mt 26:51 // Mk 14:47 // Lk 22:50).

Peter may be at a loss to know why Jesus, who has eluded capture on other occasions (7:30,44; 8:20; 10:39) and who has hidden himself when prudence required it (8:59; 12:36), should appear so willing to hand himself over to his enemies. He does not understand that the 'hour' which Jesus has spoken about so often (see 2:4; 7:30; 8:20; 12:23,27; 13:1; 17:1) has finally come.

'Put your sword into its scabbard,' Jesus tells him. 'Shall I not drink the cup that the Father gave me?' (18:11). This allusion to the agony scene in the garden, which only the Synoptic Gospels relate (Mt 26:36-46 // Mk 14:32-42 // Lk 22:40-46), highlights the voluntary character of Jesus' sufferings and death.

We should also note that, in John's Gospel, Jesus' exhortation to the wielder of the sword to refrain from violence expresses a 'theological' rather than a practical concern (cf. Mt 26:52).

Peter denies Jesus three times (18:15-18, 25-27)

We move now to the high priest's house. Peter, having survived the fracas in the garden by beating a hasty retreat (Mt 26:56 // Mk 14:50), is standing at the gate leading into the courtyard. With new-found courage, he and 'another disciple ... the acquaintance of the high priest' (18:15-16) have followed Jesus there. In the Synoptic versions, Peter is unaccompanied (Mt 26:58 // Mk 14:54 // Lk 22:54).

The Johannine text does not explicitly state that Peter's companion is the 'beloved disciple'; but, given the fact that they are paired together elsewhere (20:2-10; 21:20-23) and that the beloved disciple stood steadfastly by Jesus' cross (19:26-27), it is reasonable to assume that he is.

Day Five

This evening the post of gatekeeper is held, surprisingly enough, by a maidservant who, at the request of Peter's influential friend, admits him to the courtyard (cf. Acts 12:13). The scene is set for one of the most memorable events in the Gospel.

'You are not one of this man's disciples, are you?' she asks Peter, obviously aware of Jesus' fate. With unconscious irony he replies, 'I am not' — a cowardly response when we recall Jesus' fearless 'I am' in the garden (18:5,8). Like Jesus, Peter is also on trial.

His infidelity is highlighted as the story progresses by the evangelist's frequent use of the word 'disciple' and by the fact that Jesus' courageous stand before Annas is interposed between Peter's first and second denials (contrast the Synoptic versions). By this means, the writer also succeeds in keeping the focus on Jesus.

The questions addressed to Peter (they are somewhat less pointed than in the other Gospels) are questions which the Christians of the Johannine church must have had to answer on many occasions. There is, therefore, a pastoral relevance in the juxtaposition of the weakness of Peter and the consistent strength of Jesus.

John may be giving his community a model, both negatively and positively, of how they should behave when confronted by official Judaism.

With an eye for detail that suggests an eye-witness account and that adds a note of verisimilitude to the text, the writer tells us that the night is cold, as indeed it often is in Jerusalem in early April. The slaves and the guards and the unfortunate Peter are standing around a 'charcoal fire' (18:18) in an attempt to keep themselves warm. After the resurrection of his Lord, also beside a charcoal fire (21:9), Peter will repent of his threefold denial and will thrice affirm his love of Jesus — a nice dramatic touch.

While Peter is being questioned by nonentities outside, Jesus is being interrogated by the supreme authority within (18:19-24). Later Peter will have a similar experience when, arraigned before the Sanhedrin* for healing a crippled beggar (Acts 3:1-10), he will confront Annas and Caiaphas with conspicuous courage (Acts 4:5-22).

Peter is asked once more (not by the servant girl this time) if he is a disciple of Jesus (18:25); and, without resorting to an oath as he does in the Synoptic Gospels, he says plainly, 'I am not.' This is a far cry from his boast to Jesus, 'I will lay down my life for you' (13:37).

However, we must say this for Peter. At least, he is there. Where are the others who followed Jesus? Surely absence also bespeaks denial.

Though we have no way of knowing for certain, it is not impossible that Jesus, still bound, is being led through the courtyard on his way to Caiaphas (18:24) and is within earshot when a relative of Malchus puts the final question to Peter: 'Didn't I see you in the garden with him?' (18:26). It is this fact rather than his Galilean accent that gives him away (cf. Mt 26:73 // Mk 14:70 // Lk 22:59).

No sooner has Peter lied his way out of this predicament than the cock crows, and Jesus' prophecy is fulfilled (13:38). The disciple is surely touched to the depths of his being by this event because the prophecy was given, after the washing of his feet, in the context of Jesus' proclamation of the new commandment of love. Perhaps he now recalls his master's words: 'I give you a new commandment: love one another. As I have loved you, so you also should love one another. This is how all will know that you are my disciples, if you have love for one another' (13:34-35).

Unlike the Synoptic writers (Mt 26:75 // Mk 14:72 // Lk 22:62), John makes no mention of Peter's tearful reaction. He will highlight the fallen disciple's repentance later in a post-resurrection encounter which he alone relates (21:15-19). John's perspective is theological, not psychological.

The empty tomb (20:2-10)

The finding of Jesus' tomb empty on Easter Sunday morning is variously reported by the different evangelists. In the Johannine version, Mary Magdalen comes alone when, significantly, the land is still in darkness (20:1; cf. Mt 28:1 // Mk 16:1-2 // Lk 24:1).

She reports her discovery to 'Simon Peter and to the other disciple whom Jesus loved' (20:2; cf. Lk 24:12); and they make their way to the tomb with haste and, I suspect, with more perplexity than hope. Despite his denial of Jesus, which presumably is common knowledge, Peter is still a man of standing among the disciples.

More fleet of foot than his companion, the beloved disciple reaches the tomb first (20:4,8), Peter following, not for the first time (18:15), in his footsteps. The fact that he defers to Peter is probably best explained in terms of the special role assigned to Peter in the appendix to the Gospel (21:15-19).

There is a pattern of growth in this episode. Mary sees a stone which has been rolled away from the tomb (20:1); the beloved disciple sees the burial cloths (20:5); and Peter sees both the burial cloths and the cloth that had covered Jesus' head (20:6-7; cf. Lk 24:12).

However, it is the beloved disciple who sees and believes (20:8). The words of Jesus in the supper discourse might well be applied to him in this present context: 'Whoever has my commandments and observes them is the one who loves me. And whoever loves me will be loved by my Father, and I will love him and reveal myself to him' (14:21; cf. 1 Jn 4:7).

Peter, by contrast, does not come to resurrection faith by seeing the empty tomb but on the basis of an appearance of the Lord to him (Lk 24:34; 1 Cor 15:5). As Schillebeeckx (1981:417) states: 'There is no belief in the Resurrection without Easter grace, and an empty tomb is still not an Easter experience.'

The miraculous catch of fish (21:1-14)

At intervals of a week after this event, Jesus appears twice to his disciples in the room where they have locked themselves in 'for fear of the Jews' (20:19). Thomas is present only on the second occasion.

However, it is the third appearance of Jesus to seven of his disciples, which John alone records (21:4-23), that concerns us here. Unlike the other appearances noted in the Fourth Gospel, this one occurs not in Jerusalem but in Galilee where he first 'revealed his glory' (2:11). Peter has a special part to play in the story.

The seven have been fishing all night without success (21:5; cf. Lk 5:5) — a situation which may lead us to recall Jesus' words, 'without me you can do nothing' (15:5). Jesus appears mysteriously (unrecognised by them at first — cf. 20:14-15; Lk 24:15-16) and gives them advice which they follow. They have a splendid catch of fish (cf. Ezek 47:9-10). Eventually, and much in character (cf. 20:8), the beloved disciple recognises that it is the Lord who has intervened (21:7).

Peter, who is also the key person in the Lucan version (Lk 5:1-11), responds impulsively to this information by leaping from the boat and making for the shore (20:8; cf. Mt 14:29 — the walking on the water).

There are significant differences in these two accounts. Could it be that, in speaking of **one** boat (21:3,6,8; cf. Lk 5:2,7,11), of **one** untorn net (21:11; cf. 19:23-24; Lk 5:6) and of **one** man (Peter) hauling it in (21:11; cf. Lk 5:7), John is creating an image of the kind of unity he would like to see in his community in particular and among the disciples of Jesus in general? And is it fanciful to suggest that we have, in these details, an image of one to whom Jesus assigns a special missionary role (cf. Lk 5:10; Mt 4:19 // Mk 1:17) in a unified church?

For the second time in the Gospel, Jesus provides a meal of bread and fish by the shores of the lake (cf. 6:1-15). The link between the two events is reinforced by the fact that the same Greek word, *opsarion* (translated in 21:9, 10,13 as 'fish'), is found nowhere else in the New Testament except in 6:9,11.

Just as the disciples at Emmaus recognise Jesus in the eucharistic sign of the bread blessed and broken (Lk 24:30-31), so those by the lakeside, at the dawn of a new day (21:4), are confirmed in their faith by an experience similar to Jesus' feeding of the multitude (6:1-15).

Perhaps they recall with increased understanding Jesus' words, 'whoever comes to me will never hunger' (6:35).

The missioning of Peter the shepherd (21:15-19)

After the meal, Jesus says to Peter, who finds himself beside a charcoal fire once again (21:9; cf. 18:18), 'Simon, son of John, do you love me more than these?' (21:15; cf. 1:42). We can only imagine with what feeling Peter replies to this rather solemn question, 'Yes, Lord, you know that I love you.' This response, as Marsh (1968:672) observes, must be 'qualified by the knowledge which Peter now knows Jesus has of the disciple's heart' (cf. 13:38).

As Jesus has fed his sheep in the previous pericope*, so Peter must assume a similar role from now on. So that 'the LORD'S community may not be like sheep without a shepherd' (Num 27:17; cf. 1 Pet 2:25), Jesus tells him, 'Feed my lambs.'

Omitting the reference to 'more than these', Jesus repeats his question to 'Simon, son of John' a second and a third time (21:16-17). Peter, who is understandably distressed, replies with increasing vehemence, protesting his love for Jesus.

The risen Lord commissions him to 'tend' (21:16) and to 'feed' (21:17) his sheep. It is a task that calls for self-sacrificing love and generous service. Having learnt this lesson well, Peter will later write to the leaders of the Gentile Christian communities: 'Tend the flock of God in your midst, [overseeing] not by constraint but willingly, as God would have it, not for shameful profit but eagerly. Do not lord it over those assigned to you, but be examples to the flock' (1 Pet 5:2-3).

There is no suggestion in the above interchange that Jesus doubts the genuineness of Peter's love for him. The repetition in verses 15-17 serves as much to highlight the importance of Peter's commission as to emphasise the truth of his repentance.

In his threefold affirmation of love Peter makes reparation for his triple denial. Perhaps the evangelist intends this to be a source of encouragement for members of his church who have been less than faithful in their commitment to Jesus.

This episode continues on an ominous note with what commentators have taken since ancient times as a prophecy of Peter's death by crucifixion (21:18-19; cf. 2 Pet 1:13-15), details of which were doubtless common knowledge by the time the Gospel was written. Peter will finally make good his boast, 'I will lay down my life for you' (13:37).

By his death he will glorify God (21:19). This is an idea which Peter himself will take up in his first epistle: 'But whoever is made to suffer as a Christian should not be ashamed but glorify God because of the name' (1 Pet 5:16).

Jesus, who had responded to Peter's boast by saying, 'you cannot follow me now, though you will follow later' (13:36), now says to him, 'Follow me' (21:1; cf. 1:43). It is an invitation to imitate him in life and in death.

We will consider his enquiry about the fate of the beloved disciple (21:20-23) in another reflection.

3. *Thomas (Jn 11:16; 14:5-7; 20:24-29; 21:2)*
Introduction

Thomas, who rates nothing more than a mention in the Synoptic Gospels in the lists of the apostles (Mt 10:2-4 // Mk 3:16-19 // Lk 6:14-16; cf. Acts 1:13), has a more prominent part to play in John.

On three occasions in the Gospel he is called Didymus (11:16; 20:24; 21:2) which is the Greek equivalent of his Aramaic name and means 'the twin'. This, as Pfitzner (1988:327) surmises, may suggest 'something of the nature of the man, as well as his birth'.

A representative figure

He represents those followers of the Lord who have to overcome their doubt in order to believe. These are they for whom, as the common English idiom expresses it, 'seeing is believing', whereas, in Johannine theology, believing is seeing (that is, with the eyes of faith). Of them Jesus says, 'Unless you people see signs and wonders, you will not believe' (4:48).

According to Culpepper (1983:123), 'He is the model of the disciple who understands Jesus' flesh but not his glory. Thomas is therefore the opposite of Peter, who saw Jesus' glory but could not accept his suffering.'

Thomas who would die with Jesus (11:16)

Thomas's first words in the Gospel are uttered, after the death of Lazarus, in response to Jesus' belated invitation to the disciples to accompany him to the house of Martha and Mary (11:15). Well aware of the danger of the situation (cf. 10:31; 11:8), Thomas says, 'Let us also go and die with him' (11:16; cf. 13:37). It is the remark of a realist who, like Peter, possesses qualities of leadership.

For Bultmann (1971:400), it points to the 'blind devotion' of one who has yet to see the light. It bespeaks love or at least resignation to his fate on the part of a man who, in Lightfoot's (1960:220) words, is 'despairingly yet doggedly faithful'.

Whereas Jesus invites the disciples to come with him that they may believe (and, therefore, 'have life in his name' — 20:31; cf. 1 Jn 5:13), Thomas invites them that they may die together.

Unconsciously, he anticipates Jesus' teaching on the cost of discipleship. 'Whoever loves his life loses it,' he will hear Jesus say, 'and whoever hates his life in this world will preserve it for eternal life' (12:25; cf. 16:2; 15:12-13, 18-20; 13:36; 21:18-19; Mt 16:24-26 // Mk 8:34-37 // Lk 9:23-25). However, he is not yet at the point where he can state with Paul, 'If, then, we have died with Christ, we believe we shall also live with him' (Rom 6:8).

Thomas who would know the way (14:5)

At the beginning of his supper discourse, Jesus informs his disciples that he is going to prepare a place for them to which he will take them on his return (14:2-3). 'Where [I] am going,' he adds, 'you know the way' (14:4). It is almost a provocative statement in view of their lack of comprehension of so much related to his person and mission; and, not surprisingly, it elicits from them two questions which betray the speakers' ignorance (14:5 — Thomas; 14:8 — Philip).

'Master,' Thomas says to Jesus, 'we do not know where you are going; how can we know the way?' In reply, Jesus reveals himself as 'the way and the truth and the life' (14:6). He is the only way to that one, his Father, towards whom his entire life is oriented (see, among other texts: 4:34; 5:19,30; 8:28; 12:50; 14:10; 15:15). Indeed, as he tells Philip, 'Whoever has seen me has seen the Father' (14:9); for he and the Father are one (10:30; 17:11,21-23; cf. 8:19).

Their business, as he will later remind Peter, is to follow him (21:22).

Thomas who would see and touch the risen Lord (20:24-29)

The episode in which Thomas is granted a special apparition of the risen Lord is peculiar to the Fourth Gospel; and, like so many other events in John, it explores the theme of faith. It follows a similar literary pattern to the appearance scene in 20:19-23 (cf. Mt 28:16; Lk 24:33-34).

The doubting attitude of the disciples is reported by all four evangelists. In the Synoptic Gospels it is ascribed to them generally or, at least, to some of them (Mt 28:17; Mk 16:11,14; Lk 24:11,25,41). These writers may have an apologetic* purpose in mind; for surely early Christian preachers must have met with doubt and disbelief in some quarters when they proclaimed the resurrection of Jesus (cf. Acts 17:32).

John, who singles Thomas out, also has a pastoral purpose in mind. Jesus' words to 'the twin' express the evangelist's sentiments with regard to waverers in his own community. 'Do not be unbelieving, but believe' (20:27).

Let us not be too hard on Thomas. Nathanael had his doubts, albeit at the beginning of Jesus' ministry (1:46);

and Jesus himself entertained doubts about the accepted wisdom concerning the inferior status of women and Samaritans, the desirability of wordy prayers, and many other things.

The absence of Thomas, who is identified (rather uncharacteristically for John) as 'one of the Twelve' (20:24; cf. 6:67,70-71), may be but a literary device. John often prepares the reader for what is to come; but we are not told of his absence in the preceding pericope (20:19-23; cf. Mk 16:14).

Whatever the historical truth may be, the reported absence of Thomas is in character. It bespeaks a certain independence. Perhaps, unlike the others, he is unafraid of 'the Jews' (20:19).

In the fervour of their new-found faith, these Spirit-filled disciples joyfully preach the Good News to the sceptical one. 'We have seen the Lord,' they say (20:25; cf. 20:18); but Thomas demands tangible evidence that anything good could come out of the Nazarene's death.

The distressing image of Jesus' battered body, including the detail about the wound in the Saviour's side, which John alone mentions (19:34; 20:20,25,27; cf. Lk 24:39), is fresh in his mind. He has to reconcile this remembrance with his friends' claim. The only way to do that is to see for himself (cf. 1:46 — Nathanael), to touch Jesus as, indeed, Jesus invites his disciples to do, in words not unlike those of Thomas, in the Lucan account (Lk 24:39-40).

Of his denial, which is very emphatic in Greek, Westcott (1892:296) observes that it 'corresponds with the temper which hopes at once and fears intensely.'

As before, Jesus enters through the locked doors, stands in their midst and greets them with the same words, 'Peace be with you' (20:26; cf. 20:19). Obviously aware of the words in which Thomas has couched his doubt, Jesus directs him to touch his wounds.

Day Five

We are not told that Thomas accepts this invitation. He has no need to because he sees beyond the 'physical' reality with that God-given insight which is at the heart of Christian faith. In Marsh's (1968:646) words: 'To the almost impossibly generous invitation to the good sceptical mind he responded with something as far removed from scepticism as anything in scripture, with the words, "My Lord and my God".'

This is the highpoint of all the titles accorded to Jesus and the last of the many confessions of faith in the Fourth Gospel. It recalls the very first of these confessions, the evangelist's own, with which the Gospel begins: 'In the beginning was the Word, and the Word was with God, and the Word was God' (1:1; cf. Ps 35:23-24).

Thomas does more than merely recognise Jesus. Like the Baptist, he has 'seen and testified that he is the Son of God' (1:34). As Bultmann (1971:695) expresses it: 'Thomas has now seen Jesus in the way that Jesus wills to be seen and ought to be seen.'

In this episode and in the previous apparition stories, the evangelist is at pains to emphasise for his community (especially the waverers among them) the absolute importance of faith in Jesus — a fact which is reinforced both by the verse which concludes the chapter (20:31) and by Jesus' response to Thomas. 'Have you come to believe', says Jesus, 'because you have seen me? Blessed are those who have not seen and have believed' (20:29; cf. 1:50; 13:17).

For Westcott (1892:297), 'This last and greatest of the Beatitudes is the peculiar heritage of the later Church.' It urges Christians of subsequent generations who, like Thomas, were not present on Easter night, to proclaim faith that is not dependent on any other sign than that of the community itself vivified by the Spirit of Jesus.

To such Christians, Peter has this to say: 'Although you have not seen him you love him; even though you do not see him now yet believe in him, you rejoice with an indescribable and glorious joy, as you attain the goal of [your] faith, the salvation of your souls' (1 Pet 1:8-9).

2. PRAYING WITH PETER

Many of us will find a close similarity between our own Christian faith journey and the experience of Thomas recorded in the 20th chapter of St John's Gospel. We may well see ourselves, in the word of the Gospel, as his 'twin'. With this in mind, you may prefer to spend this session with Thomas as he makes the important steps which lead to his proclamation of Jesus as his Lord and his God. If this is the case, leave the material which follows for another occasion.

Confronted with what the French would call an embarrassment of riches, I have had to make a choice even among the episodes in which Peter features; so these few guidelines for prayer relate only to the incident in which Jesus washes the feet of his disciples. Again, may I add, please feel free to select for your prayerful reflection one of the other Petrine texts which we considered above.

Identifying with Peter, briefly recall some of the events which have brought you to this day — the invitation of your brother Andrew, formerly a disciple of the Baptist, to meet 'the Messiah' and your first encounter with the Nazarene who called you Kephas; the wedding feast at Cana; the memorable journey through Samaria; your confession of faith (perhaps over-dependent on the signs Jesus wrought) in the synagogue in Capernaum, following the miracle of the loaves and fishes; and the extraordinary event of the raising of Lazarus which provoked even more hostility on the part of the authorities than Jesus' curing of the man at the Sheep Gate or the man born blind.

Take in the scene at the table in the large upper room, furnished and prepared for a banquet, noting especially

Day Five

the pensive mood of Jesus and what appears to be a certain unease on the part of Judas.

During the meal Jesus rises from the table, casts off his outer garments, ties a towel around his waist and, having filled a basin with water, proceeds to wash the feet of your companions. You are horrified at the prospect of having your feet washed by Jesus and you give expression to your extreme reluctance as he approaches you; but he is insistent and issues what amounts to an ultimatum. Confused in mind and heart, you invite him to wash you all over, wondering where this strange behaviour will lead to.

What answer can you possibly give when Jesus asks those assembled if they understand what he has just done? What does Jesus mean by saying, 'Not all of you are clean'? What is he getting at when he says that we must wash each other's feet? It is altogether too much to take in.

Stay at the table, if you wish, until the traitor has been identified and has departed, the new commandment has been given by Jesus, and Peter has protested his willingness to die for his master.

You may like to conclude the session by making this prayer of Origen your own:

> Jesus, my feet are dirty. Come and slave for me; pour your water into your basin and come and wash my feet. I am overbold, I know in asking you this, but I dread what you threatened when you said, 'If I do not wash your feet it means that you can have no companionship with me.' Wash my feet, then, because I do want to have companionship with you.[3]

---

[3] For this prayer from Origen's *Homilies on Samuel I* (PG 13, 235D-236A) I am indebted to Geoffrey Preston (1978:78).

3. PRAYING WITH JESUS

Taking the above reading or any one of the day's readings as your starting point, pray in solitude with Jesus after the imaginative fashion suggested for other days of the retreat.

As a variant or in addition to the above, it could be fruitful to take the high priestly prayer which the evangelist places on the lips of Jesus at the conclusion of the supper (17:1-26). Listen with reverent attention as he prays it aloud and slowly, substituting your own name or some other reference to yourself whenever the pronouns 'they' and 'them' (indicating Jesus' disciples) appear in the text.

4. CONTEXTUAL PRAYER

John Navone (1986) has drawn our attention to the importance of questions in the Synoptic Gospels, especially those asked by Jesus himself which number almost one hundred (not counting parallels).

However, it is in St John's Gospel, as Wijngaards (1986:37) points out, that we find the most questions.[4] They are used repeatedly by Jesus in his teaching ministry as a way of challenging people to look more deeply into those mysteries of life and death which confront us all. Even though they are addressed in the Gospel narrative to Jesus' contemporaries, no disciple of his across the centuries can evade them.

Taking only the Petrine texts from today's readings and omitting the rhetorical utterance, 'Shall I not drink the cup that the Father gave me?' (18:11), we find three questions on the lips of Jesus: 'Do you also want to leave?'

---

[4] For an excellent treatment of this distinctive feature of the Fourth Gospel, read the chapter entitled 'Questions Designed to Last' in Wijngaards (1986:35-46).

Day Five

(6:67); 'Will you lay down your life for me?' (13:38); and 'Simon, son of John, do you love me more than these?' (21:15; cf. 21:16,17).

To the first of these questions, Peter responds with a confession of faith (6:68). He learns the true answer to the second when the risen Jesus foretells the manner of his death (21:18-19). Finally, in response to the protestations of love with which Peter replies to the third question, Jesus commissions him and calls him again to be his disciple: 'Follow me' (21:19).

These three questions, especially the last one (about which, see 14:21; 1 Jn 5:3), could form the basis of your contextual prayer today; or, perhaps more appropriately, they could be used to supplement the presumably ample agenda that has arisen from the earlier study and reflection sessions.

5. PRAYING THE MANTRA

You may find that one of the following texts, used as a mantra, is most expressive of the way in which the scripture readings have touched your heart during the day:

'You have the words of eternal life' (6:68).
'My Lord and my God!' (20:28).
'You know that I love you' (21:15).

DAY SIX

JESUS, THE MOTHER OF JESUS AND THE BELOVED DISCIPLE

1. REFLECTIVE STUDY OF THE TEXT

Introduction

It is fitting that we should conclude our period of retreat by considering the events in which the mother of Jesus and the beloved disciple appear. Apart from the Baptist, these are the only people in St John's Gospel who are not given to misunderstanding the words and deeds of Jesus and who embody most fully the faith to which the evangelist would have his community bear constant and courageous testimony and to which we aspire.

Together on Calvary, they are witnesses to the glorification of Jesus and recipients of his Spirit. This is their Pentecost event whereon they receive from Jesus a commission which redefines not only our relatedness one to another but also the covenant* relationship between God and humankind.

Just as the disciples, empowered with speech which brings unity amid diversity, are given a mission embracing 'every nation under heaven' (Acts 2:5; cf. Mt 28:18-20), so Mary is called to exercise the role of universal motherhood. The mother of Jesus of the Cana story becomes, on Calvary, the mother of the beloved disciple and of all who become, through faith, the brothers and sisters of Jesus.

The Johannine Marian texts will be the focus of the guidelines for prayer which will be included later. However, as has been stated repeatedly, the retreatant is free to base his or her prayer on any aspect of the material provided. Taking account of one's present spiritual needs, it may well be that the faith experience of the beloved disciple is more to the point.

As our introductory prayer today, let us pray Mary's canticle of grateful praise, the *Magnificat*, using the inclusive language version of Schreck and Leach (1986: 16):

> My being proclaims your greatness,
> and my spirit finds joy in you, God my Savior.
>
> For you have looked upon me, your servant,
> in my lowliness;
> all ages to come shall call me blessed.
>
> God, you who are mighty, have done great things for me.
> Holy is your name.
>
> Your mercy is from age to age toward those who fear you.
>
> You have shown might with your arm
> and confused the proud in their inmost thoughts.
>
> You have deposed the mighty from their thrones
> and raised the lowly to high places.
>
> The hungry you have given every good thing
> while the rich you have sent away empty.
>
> You have upheld Israel your servant,
> ever mindful of your mercy —
>
> even as you promised Abraham, Sarah,
> and their descendants forever.

Preliminary observations

Many characters in the Gospel of John remain unnamed, especially in the Book of Signs (chapters 1-12). We do not know, for example, the identity of the young couple at Cana (2:1-12), the man born blind (9:1-41), the Samaritan woman (4:4-42), the royal official (4:46-54), or the man at the pool near the Sheep Gate (5:1-18).

Indeed, the writer does not even mention the mother of Jesus by name; and yet, strange to relate, he is the only one of the four evangelists who records the fact that the servant whose ear Peter severed is called Malchus (18:10).

Commentators like Watty (1979) have rightly pointed to the fact that anonymity does not, of itself, cast doubt on the historicity of the characters concerned. It merely indicates that their role in the Gospel is to be sought 'in their symbolism for discipleship rather than in their historical careers' (Brown 1979:196).

Pamment (1983:364) suggests that '... John is content to use descriptions rather than names in cases where the representative character of the individual or group is important, and where naming individuals would distract us from the centre of interest in Jesus.'

With these observations in mind, we will begin this final reflection by considering the identity and role of the anonymous person whom the evangelist calls the 'beloved disciple'.

Who is the beloved disciple?

Quite a few answers have been given by scholars to this question. Without analysing the arguments for and against the suggestions they have made, we will note some of their nominations for this title: John, the son of Zebedee (cf. 21:2); John Mark (Acts 12:12); Lazarus whom, we are told, Jesus loves dearly (11:3,5,11,36); and the unnamed disciple of John the Baptist who accompanies Andrew (1:35-40).

Both Brown (1966:XCII-XCVIII) and Smalley (1978: 74-82) weigh the evidence and opt for John, the son of Zebedee. However, in a more recent work, Brown (1979:

31-34) expresses a new preference for the unnamed disciple of the Baptist.

It has also been proposed that the beloved disciple is a symbolic and idealised representation of the perfect Christian disciple. Brown accepts this point of view; but he dismisses the suggestion that he is not also an historical figure. He does so on the grounds that this does not ring true with the concern that Jesus expresses in 21:20-23 in response to Peter's question about the fate of this disciple.

My own belief is that the designation, 'beloved disciple', carries a double burden of meaning. It may be said to identify a composite character embodying both John, the son of Zebedee (a true historical eyewitness to the events of the Gospel), and an unnamed follower of Jesus who came to be the revered leader of the Johannine church (an equally trustworthy and exemplary faith witness to those same events) who, for theological reasons, is retrojected into the story of Jesus' life and death.

Whoever he may have been, it seems that he served his faith community in much the same way as the anonymous Teacher of Righteousness* served the Essene* community.

Was he the author of the Gospel?

Two verses would seem to imply that the beloved disciple and the author of the Fourth Gospel were one and the same person:

> It is this disciple who testifies to these things and has written them, and we know that his testimony is true (21:24).
>
> An eyewitness has testified, and his testimony is true; he knows that he is speaking the truth, so that you also may [come to] believe (19:35).

Even if the 'testimony' referred to in the above quotations applies to the Gospel as a whole and not merely to particular incidents, one cannot conclude that the beloved disciple was also the evangelist. The first statement is drawn from the final chapter of the Gospel (commonly believed to be a later addition from a different hand); and the second statement, one of the many authorial or editorial parentheses in the Fourth Gospel, may also belong to a later stage of the formation of the text.

The most that one might infer from these quotations is that the beloved disciple is the source behind the Gospel, the one mainly responsible for the tradition underlying it.

The role of the beloved disciple

This man is **the** representative figure of the Johannine tradition: believer, disciple, beloved, witness. As Collins (1976:132) comments:

> Within this Gospel the Beloved Disciple is the epitome of discipleship. ... In a sense, the tradition of the Fourth Gospel capsulises in the single person of the Beloved Disciple the testimony of John, the receptivity of Mary, the faith of Nathanael as well as that of the man born blind, Peter, Mary Magdalen, and Thomas.

His is the purest resurrection faith. In contrast to Peter and Mary Magdalen, he believes on seeing the empty tomb (20:8). Moreover, he is the one who recognises the shadowy figure on the shore of the lake as Jesus and who exclaims, 'It is the Lord' (21:7).

Many references suggest that there is a special intimacy between himself and Jesus (13:25). He is, one might say, a man after Jesus' own heart.

A similarly intimate relationship exists between him and the mother of Jesus (19:26-27) — a fact we will discuss in greater detail later.

Furthermore, as we noted in an earlier reflection, the evangelist, in delineating the role of the beloved disciple, usually sets him alongside Peter. They are together at the supper (13:23-25), in the high priest's courtyard (18:15-16), at the empty tomb (20:2-9), and on Lake Tiberias (21:7, 20-23). Only on Calvary is Peter notably absent.

It might appear that there is a competitive element in the Peter-John relationship or in the attitude of the Johannine community towards other groupings for whom Peter is the accepted authority figure. In this connection, Culpepper (1983:122) observes:

> If there is an anti-Petrine polemic in John, it is defensive rather than offensive in tone. In the community's gospel it is clear that there is no basis for pressing Peter's superiority over the Beloved Disciple, but there is no denial of Peter's pastoral role either.

Pamment's (1983:367) suggestion that the beloved disciple is a Gentile may throw some light on the above issue. She believes that the texts in which this respected leader figures prominently serve to identify Gentile Christianity with the significant events in the lives of Jesus' original disciples.

By making the Gentile Christians' own beloved leader a witness to these events, the evangelist highlights the fact that they were not passive recipients of the tradition but active, creative and authentic embodiments of it.

The words that Jesus addressed to Thomas might have had them specially in mind: 'Blessed are those who have not seen and have believed' (20:29).

Correcting a misunderstanding

Some of the Johannine community apparently thought that Jesus had prophesied in his post-resurrection appearance by the lakeside that their beloved disciple would live until the Parousia* — a belief that, in all probability, had been sorely tested by the disciple's death.

Peter, having heard something about his own destiny (21:18-19), is concerned on this occasion to know what fate awaits the one who has been closely associated with him during the passion and its aftermath. Referring to the beloved disciple, he says to Jesus, 'Lord, what about him?' (21:21).

Without giving a direct answer to Peter's question, Jesus replies: 'What if I want him to remain until I come? What concern is it of yours?' (21:22). This gave rise to the rumour 'that the disciple would not die' (21:23) and made it necessary for the editor to clarify the matter. Hence his comment: 'But Jesus had not told him that he would not die ...' (21:23).

In summary, then, we can say that John has sought to set the record straight concerning the early Christians' expectations of the return of Christ (cf. 2 Pet 3:4). In doing so, he has made use of the misunderstanding technique which he has employed in so many other places in his Gospel.

Mary's role in the Gospel

Mary of Nazareth appears only twice in the Fourth Gospel, in pericopes which are peculiar to John — at Cana (2:1-12) and at the foot of the cross on Calvary (19:25-27). On neither occasion does the writer refer to her by name. For him she is always 'the mother of Jesus' (2:1,3,5; 19:25,26; cf. 6:42).

Jesus himself does not call her 'mother' (*imma* in Aramaic*); but, as is his wont in speaking to women (4:21; 8:10; 20:15; cf. Mt 15:28; Lk 13:12), he addresses her as 'woman' (2:4; 19:26). While this mode of address is in no way lacking in courtesy, it is unprecedented in Greek and in Hebrew for a son to speak thus to his mother.

A plausible explanation, which takes account of the writer's penchant for symbolism, might relate this woman to Eve, the 'woman' of Genesis (Gen 2:23) and to the 'woman clothed with the sun' of the Book of Revelation (Rev 12:1-6,13-18).

What is her role in this Gospel? In what sense is she a representative figure? Despite a plethora of Marian studies, these related questions do not admit of easy answers.

We may see her as representative of those people who faithfully awaited the coming of the Messiah. For Lohfink (1985:245): 'Mary stands for the old Israel which has not yet taken the step from the fleshly family to God's family but stands on the threshold, longing for the messianic day.' He adds: 'Beneath the cross this Israel, symbolized by Mary, will be taken into the community of faith represented by the beloved disciple.'

Since the time of the Fathers*, Mary has also been considered as a figure of the Church. We will consider this image in more detail when we examine the passion narrative.

The Cana narrative (2:1-12)

Detailed commentary

In structuring his Gospel, John attaches considerable importance to the Jewish liturgical feasts, especially the Passover*. It is in the context of such celebrations and in the light of the rich symbolism that attaches to them that Jesus' teaching is given. Against this backdrop Jesus reveals the glory of God tabernacled in his very person (cf. 1:14).

Furthermore, John sometimes calculates quite deliberately the number of days involved in important phases of Jesus' ministry. Thus we are presented with the week of the Feast of Tabernacles* (7:1-10:21), the week of the passion and the crucifixion Passover (11:55-19:42), and the

Day Six

weeks of the post-resurrection appearances (20:1-18,19-25, 26-29).

However, of particular interest to us is the first week in the Johannine account of the Good News. It records the Baptist's testimony and the beginnings of our Lord's ministry (1:19-2:11) which, as will be shown below, culminates on the seventh day in the festivities of a wedding at which Jesus gives the first clear and unequivocal sign of his messianic status. As with other indications of time and duration in the Fourth Gospel, this week needs to be understood theologically rather than chronologically.

A brief but excellent theological commentary is provided for us by Thurian (1964:121) who draws a parallel between the Johannine record of the week in question and the priestly account of the creation in Genesis 1:1-2:4. He writes:

> ... [I]n a symbolic week, Christ lays the foundation of a new creation of the messianic community, the Church, by calling one by one those who will be the pillars of this new building, the Apostles; and then, the seventh day, the sign of final rest, He shares in the joy of the marriage at Cana which symbolises and pre-figures the eschatological* marriage of God with His people, the messianic banquet of the Kingdom, and He reveals His glory in the first sign of His divine Sonship.

Of more than passing interest is the fact that the next section of the Gospel (2:13-4:54), which focuses on the first of the three Passover feasts mentioned by John, is climaxed by Jesus' second Cana miracle — the healing of the son of the royal official (4:46-54).

Some commentators have suggested that the evangelist, in constructing the narrative of the wedding feast at Cana, may have adapted a pre-Johannine story recounting an episode from our Saviour's youth (cf. Lk 2:41-51) in which he performed a miracle at a family gathering, possibly in response to a request from his mother.

This may be so; but, unlike the far-fetched accounts of Jesus' early years in the apocryphal* Gospels, the Johannine story is, in Flanagan's (1978:112) words, 'staid, conservative and heavily theological in comparison.'

Flanagan (1978:111) suggests that the original version of 2:2 listed 'Jesus and his brothers' among those invited to the wedding and that the evangelist changed 'brothers' to 'disciples' to suit his own theological ends (cf. 2:11). The listing in 2:12 ('and his disciples' is probably a late editorial addition) lends some weight to his argument.

> [1]*On the third day there was a wedding in Cana in Galilee, and the mother of Jesus was there.*

As was stated above, we are not told the names of the newly married couple; and not surprisingly, given John's theological perspective, we are not given any details of the actual marriage ritual. It may be of interest, however, to note that custom required virgins to be married on Wednesdays and widows on Thursdays. The accepted practice was for the bridegroom and his friends to process to the home of the bride where the wedding would take place. This would be followed by another procession (sometimes by torchlight) to the bridegroom's house for the nuptial festivities.

The scene of this most memorable of weddings is Cana. Like Nazareth, it is a village which is not referred to anywhere in the Hebrew Scriptures; and John alone of the New Testament writers notes its existence (2:1,11; 4:46; 21:2), adding each time that it is 'in Galilee'.[1]

Mary appears to be a specially invited guest at the wedding and may well be a relative of one of the people being

---

1   The location of Cana is disputed; but the ruins of ancient Kirbet Qana (eight miles north of Nazareth) are more likely to have been the site than the village of Kafr Kenna (four miles north-east of Nazareth) which is a place of Christian pilgrimage today.

Day Six

married. Her intervention with respect to the failing wine supplies and her directive to the waiters suggest that she has an important role in the proceedings.

The phrase, 'the third day', is a particularly evocative one for Christians. Given Jesus' reference to the raising up of the temple of his body 'in three days' in the following pericope (2:19-22), it may be an example of Johannine foreshadowing; or, taking account of the four previously mentioned days (1:19,29,35,43), we may see it as completing the seven days of the new creation announced in the very first words of the Gospel — 'In the beginning ...' (1:1; cf. Gen 1:1).

Other Christian resonances may be found in those elements of Jesus' teaching in the Synoptic Gospels in which weddings figure (Mt 22:1-14 // Lk 14:16-24). Even more to the point is the fact that a nuptial celebration becomes, in the Book of Revelation, a symbol of the glorious messianic fulfilment (Rev 19:7,9). Significantly, it is 'the wedding day of the *Lamb*' (cf. Jn 1:29,36).

² *Jesus and his disciples were also invited to the wedding.*

The disciples of Jesus are not identified by name. We may suppose that they include some or all of those whose call to follow Jesus is recorded in 1:35-51. One of them, Nathanael, is a native of Cana (21:2); but neither he nor the others have any part to play in the proceedings except as witnesses to the miracle in which the glory of Jesus is revealed for the first time (2:11).

³ *When the wine ran short, the mother of Jesus said to him, 'They have no wine.'*

According to Jewish custom, marriage festivities could last for 'seven happy days' (Tob 11:18; cf Judg 14:12,17-18) or more (cf. Tob 8:20), during which time a substantial amount of wine might be consumed. It would be a humiliation and an embarrassment of major proportions for the host family if the supply failed. They would not want their wedding feast to suffer by comparison with celebrations at which they themselves had enjoyed the generous hospitality of others.

Such a situation might call to mind the striking imagery of the prophets for whom the absence of wine that gladdens the heart (Ps 104:15) was seen as a sign of God's judgment and of the impending devastation of the world. 'In the streets they cry out for lack of wine,' writes Isaiah; 'all joy has disappeared and cheer has left the land' (Is 24:11; cf. Deut 28:39).

On the other hand (and importantly for our reflection) it should be added that an abundance of wine was thought to indicate God's favour (Is 25:6; Amos 9:13-14).

Probably well into the period of celebration at Cana, Mary becomes aware of the predicament of the newly married couple. She brings the delicate situation to her son's notice, thereby setting the scene for the miracle which is to follow.

Commentators have debated whether Mary does in fact expect Jesus to perform a miracle. After all, as the evangelist states, there are no precedents for such activity on Jesus' part (2:11). Moreover, if she does expect a miracle, some direct involvement on the part of her son, why does she bother to issue a command to the servers (2:5)?

To this reader, Mary's observation, which is reminiscent of the mere statement of fact of the two sisters at Bethany (11:21,32), surely implies a request that Jesus should intervene in a way of which he alone is capable.

Thurian (1964:134) is rather more forthright and has no hesitation in asserting that 'the first words of Mary are the affirmation of a hope for such a miracle.' For him, she 'represents, at the outset of the scene, the messianic faith which will be stirred up in the disciples after the miracle.'

⁴*[And] Jesus said to her, 'Woman, how does your concern affect me? My hour has not yet come.'*

Jesus' response to Mary (literally, 'what to me and to you?') is a polite way of refusing to become involved in another's project (cf. 2 Kings 3:13). This does not imply any insensitivity to the plight of the newlyweds. His reluctance is on a much deeper level than his willingness or unwillingness to assist people in difficulty or to yield to family persuasion. Like his refusal to repeat the sign of the multiplication of the loaves (6:30-40), it reflects an awareness of what is appropriate, at a given time, to his messianic mission.

Vellanickal (1977:284) offers a good explanation for Jesus' apparently incongruous behaviour:

> But as in other instances of the Johannine miracle narratives, Jesus wants to raise the audience to a correct perspective and understanding of the significance of this miraculous intervention. Though his hour of glorification or exaltation has not yet come, it is in the light of his glorification that they have to understand this intervention.

The miracle, whereby Jesus salvages a difficult situation by changing water into wine, must be seen for what it truly is in John's theology, not simply as a wonderful event but as a *sign* which manifests the glory of Jesus (cf. 2:11) and helps to ground faith in him as 'the Messiah, the Son of God' (20:31; 11:27).

⁵*His mother said to the servers, 'Do whatever he tells you.'*

It is obvious that Mary, despite the ambiguity of Jesus' reply, expects her son to do something to rectify, or at least to ameliorate, the unfortunate state of affairs. Her words to the servers recall those of Pharaoh to the Egyptians concerning the power of Joseph to alleviate their hunger during a time of famine. 'Pharaoh directed all the Egyptians to go to Joseph and do whatever he told them' (Gen 41:55; cf. Ex 19:8). They also bring to mind her own humble response to the angel Gabriel, 'May it be done to me according to your word' (Lk 1:38).

Speaking with some authority, Mary asks for obedience to Jesus who here provides in abundance the wine that adds joy to the sealing of a marriage covenant. Later, in the midst of unspeakable sorrow, she will see her son, obedient unto death, drink the cup of suffering to the dregs as he pours out the blood of a new covenant relationship between God and humankind.

> [6] *Now there were six stone water jars there for Jewish ceremonial washings, each holding twenty to thirty gallons.*

An enormous quantity of water (and subsequently, therefore, of wine) is involved. This should not surprise us, especially in the context of a prolonged and well-attended marriage feast, because water was necessary for the ritual purifications associated with the partaking of food (cf. Mk 7:1-4).

> [7] *Jesus told them, 'Fill the jars with water.' So they filled them to the brim.* [8] *Then he told them, 'Draw some out now and take it to the headwaiter.' So they took it.*

The fact that the stone jars are filled to the brim, in response to Jesus' command, emphasises the magnitude of the miracle; but, as always in John's theology, the observable marvel is of importance only to the extent that it is perceived with the eyes of faith as a sign of God's glory present in the one through whom 'grace and truth' (1:14,17) have come into the world.

At Jesus' further command the servers take a sample of the contents of the jars to their supervisor who is, no doubt, a man of some experience.

> [9] *And when the headwaiter tasted the water that had become wine, without knowing where it came from*

> *(although the servers who had drawn the water knew), the headwaiter called the bridegroom* ¹⁰*and said to him, 'Everyone serves good wine first, and then when people have drunk freely, an inferior one; but you have kept the good wine until now.'*

There is no description of the miracle itself, of how (in the poet Richard Crashaw's words) 'The modest water saw its Lord and blushed.' With economy of detail the evangelist simply records the headwaiter's discovery and the presence of the servers who can witness to the extraordinary event that has taken place.

There is a measure of subtle irony in the suggestion that they know where the wine has come from; for, while it is literally true, it can hardly be said to convey any depth of insight on the servers' part into the heavenly nature of the gift (cf. 4:10).

Just as Jesus provides an immense quantity of bread in the scene by the lakeside (6:1-15), he makes available here in Cana an abundance of wine which, in the judgment of the headwaiter, is of superior quality.

At this point, the anonymous bridegroom, who may not even have been aware of the crisis, emerges from the background. He is gently (Schnackenburg 1968:334 suggests 'humorously') chided by the headwaiter for reserving the good wine until late in the festivities.

Read in the light of prophetic texts like Amos 9:13-14, this observation conveys much more than the sound professional advice of a knowledgeable chief steward. As McRae (1978:48) says, '[It] invites the conclusion that the Messiah is now here.'

> ¹¹*Jesus did this as the beginning of his signs in Cana in Galilee and so revealed his glory, and his disciples began to believe in him.*

The replacement of the water needed for the ceremonial washing required by the Law with a superabundance of quality wine is a sign of the inauguration of the messianic era in the person of Jesus, of the old order's giving way to the new (cf. 2 Cor 5:17). The prophetic writings speak of the coming of the Messiah in these terms (see, for example, Amos 9:13-14; Hos 14:7; Joel 4:18; Jer 31:12).[2] By means of this sign Jesus 'revealed his glory, and his disciples began to believe in him' (cf. 11:40). To acknowledge that this, rather than the answering of Mary's implied request, is the primary purpose of the miracle is not to downplay the special role of Jesus' mother.

The revised New American Bible translation speaks of the Cana miracle not as 'the first' but as 'the beginning of his signs'. This is a more literal rendering of the Greek *archē* which has its correlate in Jesus' last words on Calvary. Immediately after taking the wine offered to him there, Jesus says in the presence of his mother, 'It is finished' (19:30).

> [12]*After this, he and his mother, [his] brothers, and his disciples went down to Capernaum and stayed there only a few days.*

This statement serves to harmonise John's Gospel with the Synoptic tradition which speaks of Jesus' ministry at Capernaum (cf. Mt 4:13; Mk 1:21 // Lk 4:31).

In the following verse we are told that 'since the Passover of the Jews was near, Jesus went up to Jerusalem' (2:13) where 'many began to believe in his name when they saw the signs he was doing' (2:23).

---

2 In this connection, Flanagan (1983:13) quotes from 2 Baruch 29 which is a document almost contemporary with Jesus' era:
   '... on each vine there shall be a thousand branches, and each branch shall bear a thousand clusters, and each cluster produce a thousand grapes, and each grape produce a cor [about 120 gallons] of wine ... because these are they who have come to the consummation of time.'

Like the miracle of the loaves and fishes (6:1-15), the miracle of the water turned into wine is a Passover miracle (at least in its literary context). The fact that both of these miracles contain an allusion to Jesus' passion and death (2:4; 6:15) strengthens the case for eucharistic symbolism.

There is further food for thought in the observation of Max Thurian (1964:133) who draws our attention to the fact that 'at the end of the scene, the persons who had come separately from two different directions go out together as one.'

Mary and the beloved disciple on Calvary (19:25-27)

Detailed commentary

> 25 *Standing by the cross of Jesus were his mother and his mother's sister, Mary the wife of Clopas, and Mary of Magdala.*

After the wedding feast at Cana, Mary does not appear again in the Fourth Gospel until the last dramatic moments of Jesus' life. As Kilmartin (1963:222) perceptively remarks, 'Her absence during the public life highlights her presence on Calvary.'

John alone mentions the mother of Jesus among those witnessing the awful spectacle of our Saviour's death. In his account the women stand at the foot of the cross whereas, in the Synoptic Gospels, they observe 'from a distance' (Mt 27:55-56 //Mk 15:40-41 // Lk 23:49).

It is not immediately obvious how many women are present; but if there are four (as in the Syriac tradition), it may be the author's intention to have them parallel the four soldiers who throw dice for Jesus' tunic (19:23).

> 26 *When Jesus saw his mother and the disciple there whom he loved, he said to his mother, 'Woman, behold, your son.'*

More than filial concern is involved in the words that Jesus addresses to his mother from the cross. This is hardly the time when he would provide for Mary's future. Moreover, the fact that the beloved disciple and Jesus' mother remain anonymous among a group of named characters suggests that we should look for a symbolic interpretation, one that will highlight the messianic import of the scene.

Jesus addresses his mother first in terms which call to mind the two utterances of Pilate earlier in the piece: 'Behold, the man!' (19:5) and 'Behold, your king!' (19:14). However, it might be better to look for precedents in the prophetic writings where 'Behold!' (*ide* in Greek), as Minear (1984:144) observes, is 'often used by a prophet to accompany an authoritative disclosure of God's will.'

The importance that the evangelist attaches to these words, whereby Jesus establishes a new set of intimate relationships, is emphasised by what is stated in 19:28: 'After this, aware that everything was now finished, ...' Minear (1984:144) puts it this way: 'It may be inferred that without this episode Jesus' work would have been incomplete.'

We could see Mary as the new Eve. Just as Eve 'became the mother of all the living' (Gen 3:20), so Mary becomes, through Jesus' words to her and to the beloved disciple, the mother of all who have eternal life through faith in her son. Her physical motherhood is thus reinterpreted in relation to Christian discipleship (cf. Mt 12:46-50 // Mk 3:31-35 // Lk 8:19-21; Lk 11:27-28).

For Flanagan (1978:117):
> The most convincing explanation is that she symbolises Mother Church, exercising care over her disciple children (the Beloved Disciple is given to her as much as she to him) and, to an equal extent entrusted to their care. What we have consequently is John's picture, John's *sign*, of the birth of the Church.

> ²⁷ *Then he said to the disciple, 'Behold, your mother.' And from that hour the disciple took her into his home.*

'From that hour' is more than a simple time indication. What is significant is that this is Jesus' 'hour', the time of his glorification, the time towards which his entire ministry has been oriented. The new relationship between Mary and the beloved disciple is one of the fruits of this hour.

Mary is Jesus' gift to the disciple he loves and part of the precious spiritual legacy he leaves to all of his disciples in the person of this specially favoured one. In Flanagan's (1978:117) words: 'The Beloved Disciple must stand for all beloved disciples who will believe, follow, remain close by, and love. Their supreme gift will be to become children of Jesus' mother, therefore his brothers and sisters.'

Both the mother of Jesus and the beloved disciple are given special offices. Jesus' 'hour' is theirs as well.

Immediately after this scene, Jesus says, 'I thirst' (19:28); and he who had changed water into wine of superior quality at Cana now takes 'common wine' from a sponge mounted on a sprig of hyssop (19:29-30).

Mary hears him say, 'It is finished' (19:30); and, together with the beloved disciple, receives the gift of his spirit. To her in a special way apply the words of the prologue: 'And the Word became flesh and made his dwelling among us, and we saw his glory, the glory as of the Father's only Son, full of grace and truth' (1:14).

2. PRAYING WITH MARY, THE MOTHER OF JESUS

The fact that scholars question the historicity of the two narratives in which Mary appears should not deter us from imaginatively entering into her experience as it is there presented. While acknowledging the symbolic elements and the theological content of the pericopes in question, we may assume that John's presentation of the mother of Jesus is consistent with his community's understanding of her person and her significance.[3]

Begin by making the journey with Mary, travelling on foot from Nazareth to Cana. What are her thoughts as she makes her way (probably accompanied by some others of her townspeople) to be present at yet another wedding? Stand in her shoes as she participates in the nuptial ceremonies and in the festivities that follow.

What is her role in catering for those who have been invited to the celebration? How does she become aware of the failing supply of wine? Has a distraught host appealed to her? What are her feelings as she approaches Jesus to speak on behalf of the newly married couple?

How does she react to his apparent lack of interest in the situation? What prompts her to tell the servants to carry out any command that Jesus might give? And what emotions well up in her compassionate heart when she hears the news that a great quantity of water has been changed into wine of superior quality?

What does she have to say to her son as they slowly wend their way, in company with his brothers and his disciples, to Capernaum on the north-western shore of the Sea of Galilee? There, almost 40 kilometres from Nazareth, they will spend a few days together.

Rest awhile with your thoughts and feelings, praying as the Spirit moves you, before joining Mary on another journey — this time, the way of the cross that leads to Calvary. Stand with her, the sinless one, at the foot of the cross on which her son hangs in torment bearing the

---

[3] For a very beautiful imaginative reflection on the Cana incident, see Carretto (1986:41-46).

burden of our sinfulness. Recall the words of the prophet, 'Can a mother forget her infant, be without tenderness for the child of her womb?' (Is 49:15).

Supported by the beloved disciple, her sister, and two other women, Mary the wife of Clopas and Mary of Magdala, she looks on in anguish as the brutish Roman soldiers divide the garments of her son and as they cast lots for his seamless tunic. She hears above the clamour of the crowd Jesus' last words to her, 'Woman, behold, your son,' and the words he addresses to the beloved disciple, 'Behold, your mother.'

Remain with her as Jesus, having taken the foul wine that is offered him, says, 'It is finished.' Mary sees him breathe his last; and, before the disciple leads her away from this place of infamy, she looks on helplessly as the body of Jesus is further mutilated, his side opened by the cruel thrust of a soldier's lance.

Take care, in your reflections, to avoid the unfortunate tendency of some earlier forms of spirituality whereby the sufferings of Jesus and his mother were glorified as if they were good and pleasing to God in themselves. We are redeemed not by the sufferings of Jesus but by the constant fidelity to his Father's will which led him to embrace a prophetic way of life and to take decisions which culminated in his passion and death on the cross.

3. PRAYING WITH JESUS

One way in which we could enter imaginatively into the interior life of Jesus, in response to the Cana reading, is to walk with him and his companions from the scene of the wedding feast to the lakeside village of Capernaum. He speaks to his mother and to his disciples as they journey together; but he also communes in the depths of his being with the Father whose work he must accomplish (17:4) and whose name he must reveal (17:6).

With the manifestation for the first time at Cana of the glory he had with the Father before the world began (17:5), he has reached a turning point in his life and has taken his first step on the way of the cross that leads inexorably to Calvary.

Later he will pray for those who travel with him on this journey: 'Father, they are your gift to me. I wish that where I am they also may be with me, that they may see my glory that you gave me, because you loved me before the foundation of the world' (17:24).

Structure your time during this session as you wish. You may prefer simply to spend time with Jesus as he pours out his life on the cross with a love greater than we can conceive (cf. 15:13). Dwell on his words, 'I thirst', which, more than just a statement of painful fact, are prayerfully expressive of the same sense of missionary urgency that has characterised his whole life (cf. 4:7). Hear them as addressed to you personally, and respond.

Mindful of the great mystery they express, listen also to his final words, 'It is finished.'

A third possibility is to identify with all who are 'in Christ', especially those in whom he continues to suffer today, the least of his brothers and sisters (cf. Mt 25:40,45), and to pray with and for his Mystical Body. This could be a helpful counterbalance to our concentration over the past few days with our personal concerns.

Jesus' prayer is that we, who are branches of the one vine (15:5), may be one in heart and mind, 'a new creation' (2 Cor 5:17) born of his love and bonded by ties closer than blood relationship (cf. 19:25-27). 'I pray ... that they all may be one, as you, Father are in me and I in you, that they also may be in us ...' (17:20-21; cf. 17:11,22).

Lest we live our lives in splendid isolation, let us join our prayer with that of the impoverished and suffering Christ which rises from the throats of millions of our contemporaries, confident in the knowledge that God hears the cry of the poor.

4. CONTEXTUAL PRAYER

Obedience. Mary, the mother of Jesus, gives but one command in the four Gospels: 'Do whatever he tells you' (2:5). Expressive of the same attitude which moved her to say to the angel Gabriel, 'May it be done to me according to your word' (Lk 1:38), it enshrines one of the best pieces of spiritual advice anyone could give.

Moreover, it is reminiscent both of the formula which her people used to ratify the Covenant of Sinai, 'Everything the LORD has said, we will do' (Ex 19:8; cf. 24:3,7), and of the words whereby they renewed their commitments, 'We will serve the LORD, our God, and obey his voice' (Josh 24:24: cf. Ezra 10:12; Neh 5:12).

Obedience to what Jesus commands is the ultimate test of a disciple's love for him. In the solemn moment of his farewell discourse to his chosen ones, he says: 'If you love me, you will keep my commandments' (14:15). He then reiterates this teaching when he adds: 'Whoever has my commandments and observes them is the one who loves me' (14:21; cf. 14:23-24).

The most basic of these commandments, of course, is the one he gave them immediately after the departure of Judas in the midst of their table fellowship: 'Love one another. As I have loved you, so you also should love one another. This is how all will know that you are my disciples, if you have love for one another' (13:34-35; cf. 1 Jn 2:7-11; 2 Jn 5).

'Do whatever he tells you' is addressed to us just as truly as it was to the servants at Cana and to the members of the Johannine community. What is Jesus telling each one of us to do as we come to the end of this retreat? Let us pray about that.

Marian devotion. Writing as a Roman Catholic, I believe that one can err either by excess or by defect in the matter of Marian devotion. Though I am not prepared to take literally Bernard of Clairvaux's words, 'Concerning Mary, never enough,' I am very conscious of the fact that Mary's prophecy, 'From now on will all ages call me blessed' (Lk 1:48), has been abundantly fulfilled. She, for whom the 'Mighty One has done great things' (Lk 1:49), has been acknowledged and invoked across the centuries by the Christian faithful and has been the inspiration of some of our greatest works of art, music and literature.

In the light of that tradition, especially those enduring elements of it which relate to the spiritual maternity of Mary, we might ponder on the contemporary relevance to the Church collectively and to ourselves personally of Jesus' words, 'Behold, your mother' (19:27).

Transformation. There are many more changes effected in the Fourth Gospel than the miraculous transformation of water into wine. The most important of these are to be found in the miracles of grace wrought by Jesus in the lives of those who are open to receive the freeing truth he proclaims in word and work. We have only to think back over the stories of the representative figures that have been the subject of our reflections over the past five days.

The end of a retreat is a good time to identify the more obvious ways in which we ourselves stand in need of the life-transforming presence of Jesus. What is it, at this point in our spiritual journey, that we seem to be most in danger of running out of? Could it be the spirit of one or more of the Beatitudes (cf. Mt 5:3-10), trust in the loving-kindness of the Lord, courage and humility in the face of our recurrent sinfulness, compassion for the marginalised and despised members of society, the willingness to forgive those who have offended us, or generosity in the service of those who have special claims on our care?

Day Six

We may also need to ask whether we share the tendency of the ubiquitous 'prophets' of gloom in our Christian communities who would change the heady wine of joyful freedom in Christ's service into the insipid water of a religion based on legalism, conformism and servile fear.

5. PRAYING THE MANTRA

At the conclusion of the retreat, it may be preferable to use as a mantra the text (adapted if necessary) which has spoken to you most forcefully over the period of six days. However, if you would like to stay with today's readings, you might consider the following:

'Woman, behold, your son' (19:26).
'It is the Lord' (21:7).
'Whatever you say I will do' (cf. 2:5).

GLOSSARY

Apocalyptic literature

A highly dramatic, symbolic and visionary style of writing, rather common both before and during the lifetime of Jesus, the focus of which was the events which would accompany the last days of human history. Examples: Daniel 7-12; Revelation (Apocalypse); Mt 24-25; Mk 13; Lk 21.

Apocryphal Gospels

Writings on the life of Jesus, sometimes fanciful in character, which the early Church chose not to include in the list of books (the Canon) that make up the New Testament. For example: the *Gospel of Thomas* and the *Gospel of Peter*.

Apologetics

The area of theology which endeavours to demonstrate the reasonableness of Christian faith.

Aramaic

The Semitic language that was spoken throughout Palestine in the time of Jesus.

Canon (canonical)

A Greek word which signifies a rule, norm, yardstick or measure. With reference to the Bible, it identifies those writings which different religious communities (Jews, Protestants, Catholics, Orthodox) consider to be normative for their life of faith.

Chiasm or chiasmus

'Chiasm is a development of inclusion [see below]. Instead of simply ending and beginning in the same way, chiasm extends the balancing of the first and the last by balancing the second and the fourth (thus, abcb'a', or ab-b'a').' (Ellis 1984:10).

Christology

The branch of theology which studies the life, person, ministry and significance of Jesus, the Christ.

Concordance

An alphabetical index of the principal words of a book with a reference to the passages in which each occurs, usually with a few accompanying words indicative of the context. A classic example is Alexander Cruden's *Complete Concordance to the Bible* which was first published in 1737.

Covenant

In general, a contract or agreement between two parties which they enter into with a view to their mutual advantage. In the Bible, a bond or 'testament' between God and a person (Noah — Gen 9:8-17; Abraham — Gen 17:1-8) or a group of people (Ex 24:4-8 — the people of Israel). Christians speak of the 'new testament' that God has entered into with all humankind in Christ.

Dedication, Feast of

A feast of eight days duration beginning on 25 Kislev (during December) to commemorate the cleansing and rededication of the Temple and its altar by Judas Maccabeus in 164 B.C.E. after their desecration by Antiochus Epiphanes. As additional lights were lit in the Temple on each evening of the feast, it was also called the Feast of Lights. The Hebrew name is *Hanukkah*.

Didache

The *Didache, The Teaching of the Twelve Apostles*, is a late first century or very early second century manual of moral and liturgical instructions used in the catechesis of Gentile Christians.

Glossary

Eschatology

The area of theology which encompasses what are often referred to as 'the last things' — judgment, heaven, hell, purgatory (in some Christian denominations), the resurrection of the body, and the second coming of Christ at the end of history.

Essenes

A Jewish sect which flourished in the century before and in the century after the beginning of the Christian era. Exact in their observance of the Law, they led an ascetic life in community. Remains of one of their foundations were found at Qumran — the site of the discovery of the famous Dead Sea Scrolls.

Examination of consciousness

A structured form of reflection, the purpose of which is to nurture spiritual growth by increasing one's awareness of the ways in which God's saving grace is operative in the events of one's daily life.

Exegesis

The process/science of interpreting scriptural texts in their original context.

Fathers (of the Church)

The great theologians and teachers, both in the East and in the West, who contributed significantly to the development of the doctrinal tradition of the Church during the first eight centuries of Christianity.

Gaudium et spes

Latin for 'joy and hope', this is the title of Vatican II's *Pastoral Constitution on the Church in the Modern World*. It was promulgated on 7 December, 1965.

Gnostic

Derived from the Greek word for knowledge, *gnōsis*, it identifies both a dualistic current of thought that was widespread in the Greco-Roman world in the first two centuries of the Christian era and an ancient religious group who believed themselves to be the privileged recipients of saving knowledge. Gnosticism was the first of the Christian heresies.

Hermeneutics

The science of interpretation of a written text (or some other form of human expression); or the body of rules, principles and methods which govern its interpretation.

Inclusion

'A storyteller's technique in which what is said at the beginning of a piece is repeated at the end. The repetition forces the reader's attention back to the beginning and thus serves as a frame for the piece as a whole.' (Ellis 1984:9).

Ipsissima verba

A Latin expression which means 'the very words'. It is sometimes used in New Testament studies to identify utterances of Jesus which are believed to have been recorded and translated with complete accuracy.

Kairos

Time can be understood either quantitatively (Gk *chronos*) or qualitatively (Gk *kairos*). The former is determined by clocks and calendars (What is the time?): the latter is measured by the opportuneness of the given moment (How is the time?). A *kairos* moment has the potential to lead to a climactic revelatory experience in the life of an individual or of a community.

Kingdom of God

The term designates not a political or geographical entity but the reign, or rule, of God redemptively present in our midst through the power of the Holy Spirit. Inaugurated by Jesus and central to the mission of his Church, it is the goal (already partially realised) that God wills for the whole of Creation.

Law

The name given by the Jews to the first five books of the Bible ('the Books of Moses') or, more specifically, to the norms of conduct they contain with respect to the civil, moral, religious and liturgical life of the people. It is celebrated by the Psalmist in Psalm 119.

Glossary

Lectio divina

This Latin term (literally = 'divine reading') identifies a method of attentively reading Sacred Scripture whereby meditation on the text is intended to lead successively to spontaneous prayer and to contemplation.

Myth

Myth is used in a technical sense in this work to denote an event which has become a reference point in the experience of a community or of an individual and which is a continuing source of meaning, purpose and direction in life.

Parousia

The Greek word for 'presence' or 'arrival' which is used of the coming of Christ at the end of time.

Paschal Mystery

The great saving reality of Jesus' death, resurrection and exaltation which is celebrated at Easter (the Christian Passover).

Passover, Feast of

The Jewish festival celebrated on the 14th day of Nissan (about 1 April) commemorating the liberation of the Chosen People from their captivity in Egypt (cf. Ex 12:23-27). The Jewish name for this feast is *Pesach*.

Pentateuch

The first five books of the Hebrew Scriptures: Genesis, Exodus, Leviticus, Numbers, Deuteronomy. Also known as the *Torah* or the *Law*.

Pericope

A Greek word which literally means 'cutting all round'. Originally used to designate any passage 'extracted' from one of the classical authors, it came to mean a unit of biblical material.

Prolepsis

Theologically, the 'real anticipation' in the present of what lies historically in the future. For the writer of the Fourth Gospel, the life of glory has even now been initiated in the life of grace (cf. 6:54).

Sanhedrin

The highest governing body of the Jewish people. It numbered 71 members and was presided over by the High Priest.

Soteriology

The area of theology which focuses on the life, death, resurrection and exaltation of Jesus Christ insofar as they effect our salvation.

Synoptic Gospels

The Gospels of Matthew, Mark, and Luke which, because of their similarity in structure and content, could be read in parallel columns (synoptically).

Tabernacles, Feast of

Originally a harvest thanksgiving festival which was celebrated throughout the week of 15-22 Tishri (September/October). People lived during this time in 'tabernacles' (Hebrew = *sukkot*) made of branches — a reminder of their tent-dwelling days in the wilderness. The Temple courts were brightly illuminated by night; and the ritual provided for a solemn libation of water.

Talmud

The official commentary, incorporating a rich oral tradition, on the Jewish Law as it appears in the first five books of the Bible. It includes explanations and applications of the text and rabbinical reflections on it.

Teacher of Righteousness

The founder of the Essene community at Qumran and its spiritual guide.

Torah

The first five books of the Hebrew Scriptures. See *Pentateuch* above.

BIBLIOGRAPHY

(a) Works cited

Aschenbrenner, George. 'Consciousness Examen.' *Review for Religious* 31 (1972): 14-21.

Ashworth, Henry, ed. *A Word in Season*, I (Advent and Christmastide). Dublin: Talbot Press, 1973.

Augustine, *Confessions*. Eng. trans. R.S. Pine-Coffin. Harmondsworth: Penguin Books, 1961.

Baum, Gregory. *Religion and Alienation: A Theological Reading of Sociology*. New York: Paulist Press, 1975.

Beesing, Maria, Robert J. Nogosek and Patrick H. O'Leary. *The Enneagram: A Journey of Self Discovery*. Denville, NJ: Dimension Books, 1984.

Bligh, John. 'Four Studies in St John, I: The Man Born Blind.' *Heythrop Journal* 7 (1966): 129-44.

Brown, Raymond E. *The Gospel According to John*. Anchor Bible. 2 vols. Garden City, NY: Doubleday & Co., 1966 and 1970.

Brown, Raymond E. *The Community of the Beloved Disciple*. New York: Paulist Press, 1979a.

Bultmann, Rudolf. *The Gospel of John: A Commentary*. Eng. trans. G.R. Beasley-Smith, et al. Oxford: Basil Blackwell, 1971.

Cantwell, Laurence. 'The Quest for the Historical Nicodemus.' *Religious Studies* 16 (1980): 481-86.

Cantwell, Laurence. 'Immortal Longings in Sermone Humili: A Study of John 4:5-26.' *Scottish Journal of Theology* 36 (1983): 73-86.

Carretto, Carlo. *Blessed Are You Who Believed*. Eng. trans. Barbara Wall. Melbourne: Dove Communications, 1982.

Cassidy, Sheila. *Prayer for Pilgrims*. London: Collins (Fount Paperbacks), 1980.

Collins, Raymond F. 'The Representative Figures of the Fourth Gospel.' *Downside Review* 94 (1976): 26-46; 95 (1976): 118-32.

Collins, Raymond F. 'Jesus' Conversation with Nicodemus.' *The Bible Today* 17 n.s. (1977): 1409-18.

Collins, Raymond F. 'Proverbial Sayings in St. John's Gospel.' *Melita Theologica* 37 (1986): 42-58.

Comblin, Jose. *Sent from the Father: Meditations on the Fourth Gospel*. Eng. trans. Carl Kabat. Maryknoll, NY: Orbis Books, 1979.

Confraternity of Christian Doctrine. *The New American Bible*. Iowa Falls, Iowa: World Bible Publishers, 1970, 1986 [Revised New Testament].

Crossan, John Dominic. *The Gospel of Eternal Life: Reflections on the Gospel of St John*. Milwaukee: Bruce Publishing, 1967.

Crossan, John Dominic. *The Dark Interval: Towards a Theology of Story*. Niles, Illinois: Argus Communications, 1975.

Culpepper, R. Alan. *Anatomy of the Fourth Gospel: A Study in Literary Design*. Philadelphia: Fortress Press, 1983.

de la Croix, Paul-Marie. *The Biblical Spirituality of St. John*. New York: Alba House, 1966.

Duke, Paul D. *Irony in the Fourth Gospel*. Atlanta: John Knox Press, 1985.

Edwards, Betty. *Drawing on the Right Side of the Brain*. London: Souvenir Press, 1981.

Edwards, Tilden. *Spiritual Friend*. New York: Paulist Press, 1980.

Ellis, Peter F. *The Genius of John*. Collegeville: Liturgical Press, 1984.

Fischer, Kathleen R. *The Inner Rainbow: The Imagination in Christian Life*. New York: Paulist Press, 1983.

Flanagan, Neal M. 'Mary in the Theology of John's Gospel.' *Marianum* 40 (1978): 110-20.

Flanagan, Neal M. 'The Gospel of John as Drama.' *The Bible Today* 21 n.s. (1981): 264-70.

Flanagan, Neal M. *The Gospel According to John and the Johannine Epistles.* Collegeville Bible Commentary, no. 4. Collegeville: Liturgical Press, 1983.

Flannery, Austin, ed. *Vatican Council II: The Conciliar and Post Conciliar Documents.* Dublin: Dominican Publications, 1975.

Fiorenza, Elisabeth Schüssler. *In Memory of Her: A Feminist Theological Reconstruction of Christian Origins.* London: SCM Press, 1983.

George, Don. 'Picking the Retreat That Fits You.' *Praying* 28 (1989): 9-12.

Giblin, Charles H. 'Suggestion, Negative Response, and Positive Action in St John's Portrayal of Jesus.' *New Testament Studies* 26 (1980): 197-211.

Gillick, Lawrence. 'The Man Born Blind: A Variety of Spiritual Experiences.' *The Way* 25 (1985): 87-95.

Grenier, Brian. 'Jesus and Women.' *St Mark's Review* 119 (1984): 13-21.

Grenier, Brian. 'The Washing of the Feet: A Paradigm for Ministry.' *Word in Life* 37 (1989): 3-9.

Gula, Richard M. 'Using Scripture in Prayer and Spiritual Direction.' *Spirituality Today* 36 (1984): 292-306.

Harper, L. Alexander. 'Judas, Our Brother.' *St. Luke's Journal of Theology* 29 (1986): 96-102.

Hermisson, H.J. and E. Lohse. *Faith.* Biblical Encounter Series. Eng. trans. D. Scott. Nashville: Abingdon, 1981.

Hultgren, Arland J. 'The Johannine Footwashing (13:1-11) as Symbol of Eschatological Hospitality.' *New Testament Studies* 28 (1982): 539-46.

Keating, Charles J. *Who We Are Is How We Pray: Matching Personality and Spirituality.* Mystic, Connecticut: Twenty-Third Publications, 1987.

Kelly, Mary. 'The Pharisees and the Gospel.' *The Month* (1983): 310-317.

Kilmartin, Edward J. '"The mother of Jesus was there" (The Significance of Mary in Jn 2:3-5 and Jn 19:25-27).' *Sciences Ecclesiastiques* 15 (1963): 213-26.

Kysar, Robert. *John, the Maverick Gospel.* Atlanta: John Knox Press, 1976.

Lee, Bernard J. *The Galilean Jewishness of Jesus.* New York: Paulist Press, 1988.

Leech, Kenneth. *Soul Friend: The Practice of Christian Spirituality.* New York: Harper & Row, 1980.

Liebert, Elizabeth. 'That You May Believe: The Fourth Gospel and Structural Development Theory.' *Biblical Theology Bulletin* 14 (1984): 67-73.

Lightfoot, R.H. *St John's Gospel.* ed. C.F. Evans with the text of the revised edition. London, Oxford, New York: Oxford University Press, 1960.

Lindars, Barnabas. *The Gospel of John.* New Century Bible. Grand Rapids: W.B. Eerdmans, 1981.

Lohfink, Gerhard. 'The Miracle at Cana.' *Theology Digest* 32 (1985): 243-246.

McGann, Diarmuid. *Journeying within Transcendence.* New York: Paulist Press, 1988.

McNamara, James. *The Power of Compassion.* New York: Paulist Press, 1983.

McPolin, James. 'The Fourth Gospel and the Theme of Light.' *Scripture in Church* 6 (1976): 413-17.

McPolin, James. *John.* New Testament Message, no. 6. Wilmington: Michael Glazier, 1979.

MacRae, George W. *Invitation to John.* Garden City, NY: Doubleday (Image Books), 1978.

Marsh, John. *John.* The Pelican New Testament Commentaries. Harmondsworth: Penguin Books, 1968.

Martyn, J. Louis. *History and Theology in the Fourth Gospel.* Rev. ed. Nashville: Abingdon Press, 1979.

Michael, Chester P. and Marie C. Norrisey. *Prayer and Temperament: Different Prayer Forms for Different Personality Types.* Charlottesville, Virginia: The Open Door, 1984.

Minear, Paul S. *John: The Martyr's Gospel.* New York: The Pilgrim Press, 1984.

Bibliography

Morneau, Robert F. *Mantras for the Evening: The Experience of Holistic Prayer.* Collegeville, Minnesota: Liturgical Press, 1982.

Moule, C.F.D. 'The Meaning of "Life" in the Gospel and Epistles of St John [A Study in the Story of Lazarus, John 11:1-44].' *Theology* 78 (1975): 114-25.

Navone, John. 'The Dynamic of the Question in the Gospel Narrative.' *Milltown Studies* 17 (1986): 75-111.

Neyrey, Jerome H. 'Jacob Traditions and the Interpretation of John 4:10-26.' *Catholic Biblical Quarterly* 41 (1979): 419-37.

Neyrey, Jerome H. 'John III — A Debate over Johannine Epistemology and Christology.' *Novum Testamentum* 23 (1981): 115-27.

O'Day, Gail R. *The Word Disclosed.* St Louis, Missouri: CBP Press, 1987.

O'Day, Gail R. 'New Birth as New People: Spirituality and Community in the Fourth Gospel.' *Word and World* 8 (1988): 53-61.

Painter, John. *John: Witness and Theologian.* London: SPCK, 1975.

Pamment, Margaret. 'The Fourth Gospel's Beloved Disciple.' *Expository Times* 94 (1983): 363-67.

Pfitzner, V.C. *The Gospel According to St John.* Chi Rho Commentary. Adelaide: Lutheran Publishing House, 1988.

Preston, Geoffrey. *God's Way to Be Man.* London: Darton, Longman and Todd, 1978.

Russell, Letty M. *Becoming Human.* Philadelphia: Westminster Press, 1982.

Schillebeeckx, Edward. *Christ: The Experience of Jesus as Lord.* New York: Crossroad, 1981.

Schnackenburg, Rudolf. *The Gospel According to St John.* Vol. 1. Eng. trans. Kevin Smyth. London: Burns & Oates, 1968.

Schneiders, Sandra M. 'The Foot Washing (John 13:1-20): An Experiment in Hermeneutics.' *Catholic Biblical Quarterly* 43 (1981): 76-92.

Schneiders, Sandra M. 'God's Word for God's People.' *The Bible Today* 24 n.s. (1984): 100-106.

Schneiders, Sandra M. 'Born Anew.' *Theology Today* 44 (1987a): 189-96.

Schneiders, Sandra M. 'Death in the Community of Eternal Life: History, Theology, and Spirituality in John 11.' *Interpretation* 41 (1987b): 44-56.

Schreck, Nancy, and Maureen Leach. *Psalms Anew: In Inclusive Language.* Winona: Saint Mary's Press, 1986.

Segovia, Fernando F. 'Peace I Leave with You; My Peace I Give to You: Discipleship in the Fourth Gospel.' In *Discipleship in the New Testament*, ed. Fernando F. Segovia. Philadelphia: Fortress Press, 1985.

Sellner, Edward C. *Mentoring: The Ministry of Spiritual Kinship.* Notre Dame, Indiana: Ave Maria Press, 1990.

Sheldrake, Philip. *Images of Holiness: Explorations in Contemporary Spirituality.* London: Darton, Longman and Todd, 1987.

Simons, George F. *Keeping Your Personal Journal.* New York: Paulist Press, 1978.

Smalley, Stephen S. *John: Evangelist and Interpreter.* Exeter: The Paternoster Press, 1978.

Suggit, J.N. 'Nicodemus — the True Jew.' *Neotestamentica* 14 (1981): 90-110.

Teresa of Avila. *The Complete Works of Saint Teresa of Jesus.* Translated and edited by E. Allison Peers. 3 vols. London and New York: Sheed and Ward, 1946.

Thurian, Max. *Mary, Mother of All Christians.* Eng. trans. Neville B. Cryer. New York: Herder and Herder, 1964.

Townroe, John. 'Retreat.' In *The Study of Spirituality*, ed. Cheslyn Jones, Geoffrey Wainwright, and Edward Yarnold. London: SPCK, 1986.

Vellanickal, M. 'The Mother of Jesus in the Johannine Writings.' *Biblebhashyam* 3 (1977): 278-97.

Watty, W.W. 'The Significance of Anonymity in the Fourth Gospel.' *Expository Times* 90 (1979): 209-12.

Weber, Hans-Reudi. *Experiments with Bible Study.* Geneva: World Council of Churches, 1981.

Westcott, B.F. *The Gospel According to St John.* London: John Murray, 1892.

Wijngaards, John. *The Gospel of John & His Letters.* Wilmington: Michael Glazier, 1986.

(b) Works consulted (select list only)

Barrett, C.K. *The Gospel According to St. John: An Introduction with Commentary and Notes on the Greek Text.* 2nd ed. London: SPCK, 1978.

Billings, J.S. 'Judas Iscariot in the Fourth Gospel.' *Expository Times* 51 (1939-40): 156-57.

Brown, Raymond E. et al. *Peter in the New Testament.* New York: Paulist Press, 1979b.

Bruce, F.F. *The Gospel of John.* Grand Rapids: Eerdmans, 1983.

Collins, Raymond F. 'Mary in the Fourth Gospel: A Decade of Johannine Studies.' *Louvain Studies* 3 (1970): 99-142.

Cook, Michael. 'Jesus and the Pharisees: The Problem as It Stands Today.' *Journal of Ecumenical Studies* 15 (1978): 441-60.

Domeris, William, and Richard Wortley. *Portraits of Jesus: John.* [A Contextual Approach to Bible Study]. London: Collins, 1988.

Gula Richard M., 'Using Scripture in Prayer.' *Christian Initiation Resources* [Catechumenate — L], 1984. 1-8.

Martini, Carlo. *The Ignatian Exercises in the Light of St. John.* Eng. trans. Joseph Gill. Anand, India: Gujorat Sahitya Prakash, 1981.

Maynard, A.H. 'The Role of Peter in the Fourth Gospel.' *New Testament Studies* 30 (1984): 531-48.

Morris, Leon. *The Gospel According to John.* The New International Commentary on the New Testament. Grand Rapids: Eerdmans, 1971.

Morris, Leon. *Reflections on the Gospel of John.* Grand Rapids: Baker Book House, 1986, 1987.

O'Day, Gail R. *Revelation in the Fourth Gospel.* Atlanta: John Knox Press, 1986.

Okure, Teresa. *The Johannine Approach to Mission: A Contextual Study of John 4:1-42.* Tubingen: Mohr, 1988.

Taylor, Michael J., ed. *A Companion to John: Readings in Johannine Theology.* New York: Alba House, 1977.

Winter, Art. 'The Retreat Rainbow.' *Praying* 28 (1989): 5-8, 29-30.